Combat Uniforms of the Civil War

Colonel Ulric Dahlgren (standing) on the staff of General Mead is with Lt Col Dickinson in the straw hat, who is assistant to General Hooker. Also with them on the left, is Major General Ludlow and Lt Officer Rosenkrans a Swedish officer on a leave of absence. The soldier in foreign uniform is Count Zeppelin, a Prussian offier on a visit to the battlefields.

$20—

Combat Uniforms of the Civil War

Volume Three
The Confederate Army

Mark Lloyd
Illustrated by Mike Codd

Chelsea House Publishers
Philadelphia

Published in 1999 by
Chelsea House Publishers
1974 Sproul Road, Suite 400
P.O. Box 914
Broomall, PA19008-0914

Printed in China

Library of Congress Cataloging-in-Publication Data

Lloyd, Mark 1948-
    Combat uniforms of the Civil War / Mark Lloyd:
Illustrated by Mike Codd.
        p. cm.
        Includes index.
    Summary: Describes the military uniforms worn by
individual units of Federal and Confederate armies during the
Civil War as well as the battlefield activities of these units.
        1. United States. Army—Uniforms—Juvenile literature.
2. Confederate States of America. Army—Uniforms—
Juvenile literature. 3. United States—History—Civil War,
1861-1865—Juvenile literature. [1. Military uniforms. 2.
United States. Army. 3. Confederate States of America. Army.
4. United States—History—Civil War, 1861-1865.] I. Codd,
Michael, ill. II. Title.
UC483.L55   1998
355. 1'4'0973—dc21   98-18187
                                                  CIP
                                                  AC

        ISBN 0-7910-4993-0 (vol. 1)
        ISBN 0-7910-4994-9 (vol. 2)
        ISBN 0-7910-4995-7 (vol. 3)
        ISBN 0-7910-4996-5 (vol. 4)
        ISBN 0-7910-4992-2 (set)

Contents

Bombproofs and Confederate defenses in front of Atlanta, Georgia. In possession of Union troops.

THE CONFEDERATE ARMY

Few Southerners sought open confrontation with the Federal government. By 1860 they had developed their own unique lifestyle and simply demanded the right to be left in peace. The vast majority did not own slaves – indeed many quietly accepted the inevitability of eventual abolition. Only three countries in the Americas – Brazil, Cuba and the United States – continued to practice slavery, and it was clear to all but the most reactionary that this status quo could not continue forever. However, as the powerful northeastern states fell increasingly under the influence of European immigration, the gulf between the North and South grew until eventually many Southerners began to believe that nothing short of total independence could protect their way of life. Southern leaders began to argue that the Union of 1789 was no more than a contract between each state and the Federal government, which could be rescinded by either party. The rights enshrined in the Declaration of Independence had, they argued, never been surrendered, and in consequence, each state had the option of going its own way should it for any reason find the actions of the central government unacceptable.

In 1861, 11 states exercised this option, seceded from the Union and formed themselves into a new nation which they named the Confederate States of America. Almost at once they denied the theory on which their own creation was based: at the Montgomery Convention which followed, they declared the Confederacy to be a "permanent government" from which none had the right to withdraw. When Washington threatened to restore Federal rule by force of arms, Southerners flocked to the cause of the fledgling government. Many officers – including Robert E. Lee, who had earlier been offered command of the Union forces ordered to suppress the rebellion – resigned their commissions and offered their services to the Confederacy.

Southerners believed – and many Northerners agreed – that their way of life gave them a great advantage over the enemy. Their tradition of military service was strong, their rural lifestyle meant that most were natural horsemen and excellent shots, and their leaders possessed powers of man management born of generations of slave owning. They went to war in 1861 with an arrogance resulting as much from a belief in themselves as in their cause.

As was the case with the Union, volunteers flocked to the states rather than the central government to offer their services. Although the Confederacy initially did not introduce formal dress regulations (with the notable exception of a few regiments), most of the troops were issued with vaguely similar uniforms. Louisiana, with its strong French traditions, produced a number of Zouave units, notably the Louisiana Tigers with their striking striped pantaloons. New Orleans fielded the lavishly attired Washington Artillery and South Carolina the Charleston Light Dragoons with their European-style plumes and epaulettes, but most wore some vestige of gray.

More than any other fighting unit, the Confederate cavalry epitomized the South's attitude to war. Each man supplied his own horse and tackle, only established horsemen were accepted, and conventional military discipline was kept to a minimum. For two years the cavalry swept all before it, gaining a reputation for invincibility which led to complacency and, ultimately, to its undoing. At Brandy Station it met a new generation of Northern cavalry: well trained, well equipped and, above all, drilled in the art of modern warfare. The Southern cavalry suffered the first in a series of defeats which sent shock waves reverberating through the Confederate military command. At Gettysburg, the North, which had always enjoyed a vast industrial and numerical superiority, proved that it was now at least the equal of the South in tactics and leadership. From then to the inevitable surrender at Appomattox two years later, the South could do no more than engage in a series of delaying and rearguard actions in the hope of foreign intervention or a qualified peace.

It was during this period that the ordinary Confederate soldier came into his own. Invariably hungry, his clothing in tatters and often inadequately armed, he fought tenaciously for every inch of his land. As uniforms wore out or were destroyed in the fighting, soldiers whose homes were not under the control of the advancing Union armies asked their families for civilian replacement clothing. Others simply looted the bodies of the Union dead or stole from prisoners of war. By 1864 few Confederate regiments retained any outward semblance of order although, as the Union forces frequently discovered to their cost, their fighting spirit remained unabated. Butternut replaced gray as the color of the day as conventional dyes became all but impossible to obtain. Inevitably some troops went too far in their use of captured equipment, and at one stage the Union had to threaten to shoot as spies any enemy troops captured wearing Federal clothing. Indeed a few even abandoned uniforms completely, forming themselves into bands of bloodthirsty irregulars, although fortunately such instances were comparatively rare.

In many ways, the Confederate army was an enigma. Highly motivated, it shunned internal politics. Suspicious of any outward manifestation of class (many soldiers refused to salute officers whom they regarded as equals in the struggle for independence), it displayed to the bitter end an unwavering loyalty to its leaders in general and to Robert E. Lee in particular. A lesser army would have disintegrated when defeat became inevitable. Instead the Confederates remained a cohesive force even when denied the cohesive factor of proper uniforms. After the war many Southern troops joined the newly reformed Union army, in numerous instances gaining high office within its ranks. Today the South can boast a higher number of senior army officers *pro rata* than any other quadrant of the United States – proof that the fighting spirit of the 1860s, which enabled an ill-equipped, poorly armed and vastly outnumbered army to survive four years of bloody warfare, did not die at Appomattox.

ROBERT E. LEE

Socially, politically, and culturally, Robert E. Lee was the complete antithesis of his rival in war and one-time companion Ulysses S. Grant. Born in 1807, the fourth son of "Light Horse Harry" Lee, a veteran cavalry leader during the Revolutionary War and former Governor of Virginia, Lee could trace his ancestory through many of the great original families of America, including that of George Washington. Although Lee had married well and despite his aristocratic connections, he was not in fact a rich man. His somewhat eccentric father had an advanced sense of honor but little financial acumen and, dying when Lee was still relatively young, left a widow and seven children with a social position but without the necessary resources to maintain it. His son Robert was deeply influenced by his gentle and dignified mother, adopting many of her characteristics in later life. Above all, he gained from her a desire to excel at whatever he did.

Unable to afford a university education, Lee obtained a place at West Point from which he graduated second in his class, having been appointed corps adjutant, the highest honor available to an officer cadet. Commissioned into the elite Engineering Corps in 1829, Lee later transferred to the cavalry in search of promotion but found little to inspire him in the peacetime army. During the Mexican War (1846–48), he served as a captain on the staff of General Winfield Scott, during which time it is more than likely that he had his first encounter with Grant. Unlike the latter, who then returned to anonymity, Lee concluded the war with one wound, three brevets for gallantry, and a mushrooming reputation which prompted General Scott to describe him as "the very best soldier I ever saw in the field."

As Superintendent of West Point between 1852 and 1855, Lee continued steadily to enhance his reputation. In October 1859, while on compassionate leave at his home in Arlington, Virginia, he was ordered to Harpers Ferry to suppress a pro-secessionist insurrection led by the tempestuous John Brown. The latter's ill-conceived capture of the Federal arsenal and armory was contained by the time that Lee and the company of Marines under his command reached the area, leaving him with little to do but make a final and virtually bloodless assault on the thoroughly confused and demoralized abolitionists. The fact that the insurrection had been led by a group of whites made Lee realize that open confrontation could not be avoided for long. Avidly anti-secessionist and a non-slave owner himself, this placed Lee on the horns of a dilemma.

He had returned to his command in Texas when, on 1 February 1861, that state became the seventh to secede, and the state government ordered all Federal troops to vacate its lands forthwith. Now devoid of a command, Lee returned to Arlington to await events in Virginia. On 18 April, at the instigation of General Scott, Lee was ordered to Washington and offered command of an army then being formed to return the seceded states to the Union. Bitterly opposed to civil war, Lee refused, stating that "he could take no part in an invasion of the Southern states." When Lincoln called on Virginia to furnish troops for the invasion, the state legislature refused and instead joined the secession. Lee resigned from the army which he had served faithfully for 36 years and at once offered his services to the defense of his homeland.

Surprisingly, Lee was not initially given field command but instead was appointed military adviser to the Confederate President Jefferson Davis, in which role he was able to plan a cohesive defense for the Confederacy. Working in unison with Thomas (later "Stonewall") Jackson, he spent the early part of 1862 putting together a strike force from a number of static garrisons in northern Virginia, using it to excellent effect in an audaciously conceived attack into the Shenandoah Valley. Fearful of the threat to Washington, Lincoln was forced to hold back General McDowell's large corps for the defense of the capital, denying McClellan and the Army of the Potomac sufficient troops to execute an encircling movement around Richmond.

On 31 May 1862, General Joseph Johnston, in command of the Confederate field forces, was seriously wounded. Lee was appointed in his place and at once set about rebuilding the Army of Northern Virginia into one of the most potent fighting units of the war. Discipline and command were tightened, morale improved, and control returned to headquarters. Not willing to surrender the initiative, Lee linked with Jackson to the north, and, in a series of bloody skirmishes known

General Robert E. Lee resplendent in the uniform of a Confederate Lieutenant General. This photograph was taken by Matthew Brady in 1865.

collectively as the Seven Days' Battles, inflicted a humiliating defeat on the Union forces. For bringing the Confederacy its first major victory since Manassas (Bull Run) and for halting the Federal advance on Richmond, Lee became universally acclaimed in the South and the subject of much veneration among his own troops.

Ever a realist, Lee knew that he could not hope to beat the North in a conventional war. Instead he spent the next two years trying to keep the enemy from the industrial heartland of Richmond and from the rich farmlands of northern Virginia, at least while the crops were being harvested. In an attempt to destroy the Federal will to win, and in the hope of attracting European support for the Confederate cause, Lee embarked on a series of battles in which he relied on speed, initiative, and the sheer motivation of his men to defeat the vastly more powerful enemy. Twice expelling the Federals from his beloved Virginia, Lee won notable vic-

tories at the 2nd Battle of Manassas (Bull Run) on 29–30 August 1862, at Fredericksburg on 13 December 1862, and at Chancellorsville on 1–6 May 1863 when, outnumbered by more than two to one, he split his forces and encircled the enemy. In an attempt to shift the battlefield from the Confederacy, and with a view to enlisting support from Southern sympathizers, Lee crossed into Maryland but met overwhelmingly superior forces at Antietam (Sharpsburg) and was forced to retire back across the Potomac.

Conscious of the stalemate in Virginia and unable to influence the series of Confederate reverses in the West in the summer of 1863, Lee once again advanced into the North in a last desperate attempt to carry the war to the enemy – this time into Pennsylvania. However, unlike the Federals who had the luxury of constant reinforcements, Lee was unable to replace his losses. His veteran troops were exhausted, and many of his finest subordinates lay dead – notably "Stonewall" Jackson, killed by mistake by his own troops at Chancellorsville. Inevitably Lee was defeated at Gettysburg (1–3 July 1863), and his dejected troops were forced to retire once more behind their own defensive lines.

In May 1864, Grant assumed overall command of the Union forces and began a relentless two-pronged drive into the Confederacy. Overwhelmed by superior numbers, Lee could do little but fight a series of delaying actions, all of which only served to deplete his already scarce resources. The Confederates fought valiantly during the Wilderness campaign, at Spotsylvania, and at Cold Harbor, inflicting over 50,000 casualties on the enemy, but to no avail. Eventually Lee was forced to deploy the remnants of his exhausted troops in defensive positions outside the remaining strongholds of Richmond and Petersburg to await the inevitable outcome. Even then, for nearly a year Lee's brilliantly engineered defensive works frustrated every attempt to storm them.

The end came on 2 April 1865 when the defensive lines surrounding Richmond broke under a massive assault, forcing the remaining defenders to leave the protection of their trenches and make a last desperate break for freedom. On 9 April, Lee accepted the inevitable and surrendered his army to Grant at Appomattox Courthouse, an ordeal made easier by the magnanimity of Grant and his staff.

After the war, Lee spent several months recuperating from the rigors of the final retreat, although he never fully recovered his health. Conscious of the need to provide for his wife and seven children (the Arlington plantation that his wife had inherited had been confiscated by the Union) and mindful of the need for setting a good example to the thousands of unemployed soldiers, he accepted the position of president of Washington College (now Washington & Lee University) in Lexington, Virginia. As well as being a progressive and enlightened lecturer, Lee also placed the college on a sound commercial footing, instilling a sense of purpose into its students, many of them former soldiers from his Army of Northern Virginia.

Robert Edward Lee died in his home at Washington College in 1870 at the age of 64, and now lies buried in its grounds.

Lee, in the company of his staff, surveys the battlefield at Fredericksburg. Note the comparative simplicity of his dress compared to that of his subordinates.

Although Lee traditionally favored long cavalry boots and a large utilitarian black hat, both shown here, it was not until after Gettysburg that he began to appear regularly in the full uniform of a Confederate States general. Even then he invariably kept the adornments of rank to a minimum.

9

THE LOUISIANA TIGERS

Louisiana was never naturally a part of the United States. Initially settled by the French, it remained part of their empire until 1803, when the Louisiana Territory (which extended from the Mississippi to the Rockies) was purchased by Thomas Jefferson from the impecunious revolutionary government for $15 million. Fifty years later, the bulk of the citizens of the state of Louisiana (which had been admitted to the Union in 1812) remained insular, refusing to abandon either their traditional ways or, in the case of those in the southern part, their highly personalized Creole dialect. Few felt any allegiance to Washington, D.C. or the Federal government. Many settlers had, however, gained considerably from the growth of New Orleans as a major seaport and from the resultant increase in agricultural productivity within the state's hinterland, and they were determined to protect their new-found affluence. When therefore Louisiana seceded from the Union on 26 January 1861, they gave the newly formed Confederacy their absolute support.

The harsh realities of war came quickly to Loui-

Starke's Louisiana Brigade storming the Federal lines near "Deep Cut." Stones replaced muskets when the ammunition ran out.

siana. Within weeks of the attack on Fort Sumter, the Union navy began a highly successful blockade of the Gulf ports, effectively starving the South of most of its imports. In April 1862, New Orleans was attacked, forced to surrender, and placed under a strenuous regime of martial law designed to break, once and for all, the spirit of rebellion in the area. General Benjamin Butler, appointed military governor of the city on 1 May 1862, said:

> I find the city under the dominion of the mob. They have insulted our flag – torn it down with indignity. This outrage will be punished in such a manner as in my judgment will caution both the perpetrators and abettors of the act, so that they shall fear the stripes if they do not reverence the stars of our banner.

Within weeks, Butler had hanged a prominent citizen for removing the Union flag from a public building, had passed a law classifying as a prostitute any woman who by her actions, manner, or deeds in any way attracted the attention of the occupying forces, and had brought the British government to the brink of intervention on behalf of the Confederacy.

Headdress: Many Louisiana regiments favored the straw hat, often inscribed with patriotic logos, rather than the originally issued red stocking cap.

Trousers: Whereas most regiments abandoned the bright red shell jackets, nearly all retained the striking red, white and blue striped pantaloons reputedly manufactured from bed-ticking.

Gaiters: White leather gaiters were issued to all enlisted men and were worn throughout the war.

More fundamentally, he had hardened the resolve of the entire population of Louisiana to fight to the finish rather than yield to Northern domination.

Most volunteers joined one of the numerous independent regiments which were formed into two brigades within the Army of Northern Virginia. The first, officially designated the 8th Brigade of General Dick Ewell's Division, was commanded by Dick Taylor, the son of Zachary Taylor, 12th President of the United States, and, according to a leading critic, "the one Confederate general who possessed literary art that approached first rank." Taylor had been educated in Edinburgh and France and at Harvard and Yale before taking over the administration of his plantation in Louisiana. Pro-secession, he was appointed commander of the 9th Louisiana but failed to see action at the 1st Battle of Manassas (Bull Run). Appointed brigadier on 21 October 1861, he was given command of the Louisiana Brigade under Jackson in the Shenandoah Valley campaign and during the Seven Days' Battles. Although ill during the final stages of the latter, he showed his true grit and determination by directing his troops from the back of an ambulance. Promoted major general in July 1862, he was given responsibility for the defense of western Louisiana, halting Bank's advance in the Red River campaign of 1864. In May of that year, Taylor was further elevated to the rank of lieutenant general and given the responsibility of protecting eastern Louisiana, Mississippi, and Alabama – a hopeless task which he performed to the very best of his ability until the very end, after which he surrendered with honor rather than inflict further suffering on his troops.

The brigade itself, one of the finest in the Confederate army, comprised Seymour's 6th Louisianas, Hay's 7th, Kelly's 8th, Stafford's 9th and Roberdeau Wheat's Louisiana Special Battalion whose nickname, the "Tigers," was eventually adopted by the entire brigade. The 2nd Louisiana Brigade, comprising the 2nd, 9th, 10th, 15th, and, later, the 1st and 14th Regiments, was commanded by Brigadier Stafford until his death on 5 May 1864 during the Wilderness campaign, after which the remnants of both brigades were merged.

Whereas Louisiana troops tended to be better equipped than most in the Confederacy, they did not enjoy a statewide uniform. Troops raised in the immediate vicinity of New Orleans tended to wear a predominantly blue uniform, often with a red flannel stripe attached to the left shoulder to differentiate them from soldiers of the Union army. Rural companies, however, favored gray trimmed in a variety of colors.

Many of the original volunteer regiments remained true to their French heritage and adopted Zouave or *chasseur* uniforms. The Confederate State Zouaves (St. Leon Dupeire's Louisiana Infantry), the Louisiana Zouaves and the Zouaves and *chasseurs* all vied with each other during the first few months of the war to create the most stunning uniforms with no thought paid to their obvious impracticality in the field. The 1st Battle of Manassas however, brought home to all concerned the realities of war, and by early 1862, Taylor was able to boast a brigade "over three thousand strong, neat in fresh clothing of gray with white gaiters,

bands playing at the head of their regiments."

One of the most distinctive of the early uniforms was that issued to the Louisiana Special Battalion – the original "Tigers." It was essentially a typical Zouave costume, consisting of a red stocking cap with a blue tassel, a dark brown jacket with red braid in one of a number of patterns, and a red shirt decorated with several sashes. The colorful trousers – either blue with white stripes or a mixture of red, white and blue – were made from bed-ticking and earned the regiment its unusual nickname. The heavy jacket was often discarded in battle, enabling the troops to fight in their shirtsleeves, while the stocking cap was invariably replaced by a more popular wide-brimmed straw hat, itself often inscribed with such patriotic mot-

toes as "Tigers Win or Die," "Tiger Looking for Old Abe," and "Tiger Always." To add to the mystique of the regiment, each company had its own exotic title. Thus Company "A" became "Walker Guards," Company "B" "Tiger Rifles," Company "C" "Delta Rangers," Company "D" "Catahoula Guerrillas" or "The Old Dominion Guards," and Company "E" "The Wheat Life Guards."

The 7th Louisiana – nicknamed "The Pelicans" because of the design of the state seal often borne on their waist-belts – was another Zouave unit although, in this instance, the officers exchanged the conventional sleeved waistcoat for a shell jacket with a standing collar and badges of rank sewn on the sleeves. Available photographs of Zouave units show the enlisted men wearing con-ventional black boots or shoes protected by calf-length white gaiters, occasionally of leather but more usually of webbing.

In the best Zouave tradition, many of the regiments (including "The Tigers") recruited *vivandières*, or female sutlers, to accompany them. Such women usually wore short wool jackets of the same color and trim as those of the men, wide-brimmed plumed hats, and heavy skirts over trousers made of wool below the hemline and cotton above. Unlike their European equivalents, who often had an unenviable reputation for promis-cuity, the Southern *vivandières* were well respec-ted. Many placed themselves in the line of fire to bring water and administer first aid to the woun-ded, and several were killed.

The Louisiana Brigade fought tenaciously, if against hopeless odds, during the Battle of Spotsylvania.

CONFEDERATE INFANTRY: 1862

The Army of Northern Virginia was one of the finest fighting forces of the 19th century. Constantly outnumbered, ill-equipped, and usually hungry, it held the Union steamroller at bay for three long years before eventually yielding to overwhelming force.

The Army had its roots in the far smaller and less sophisticated Army of the Shenandoah formed in early 1861 to defend the Confederacy against Union intervention. Initially most troops were supplied, armed, and equipped by the individual states, all of which introduced their own standards of dress and uniform. As the war intensified, the unsophisticated state administrations were simply overwhelmed, necessitating central government intervention, but by then thousands of troops had been organized into a mass of regiments, battalions, and even independent companies. Some – notably the 1st Virginia Regiment, the Washington Artillery of Louisiana, and the Clinch Rifles of Georgia – had been formed, fitted out, and trained well before the war and were thus able to offer themselves to the Confederacy as fully competent fighting entities. Others, such as the Georgia Hussars who spent $25,000 on their initial outfits, lacked military training but at least had the financial ability to insure that they went to war equipped with the best (and gaudiest) that money could buy.

The Confederate government tried to equip the thousands of volunteers who enlisted in the spring and summer of 1861 for an initial period of 12 months, but gave up when it realized the impossibility of the task. Instead, volunteers were given a basic equipment list and ordered to furnish their own clothes. Potential cavalrymen were even expected to provide their own mounts, saddles, and tackle. This led to an inevitable, if unfortunate, feeling of superiority among the urban units (many of which were equipped by local subscription) when they compared themselves to their less affluent country cousins.

An attempt was made during the summer of 1861 to bring a degree of uniformity to the Confederate ranks. Many states had based their own local uniforms on existing U.S. army patterns, with the result that a disconcertingly large number of Southern troops were still clothed almost exclusively in Federal blue. When this had led to confusion in the ranks, such as during the 1st Battle of Manassas (Bull Run), the South had invariably gained, but its legislators were realistic enough to know that this would not always be the case and strove to introduce as soon as possible a drab gray uniform. Certain of the more outlandish units, notably the Zouave regiments, initially showed a marked disinclination to relinquish their bright

The Confederate Infantry withstands a massed Federal attack during the Battle of Fair Oaks, 31 May 1862.

Jacket: Issue gray double-breasted tunics were unpopular and were usually replaced with civilianized gray single-breasted jackets.

Side arms: Whole units abandoned the bayonet in favor of privately acquired hunting and Bowie knives. These were subsequently found to be totally inadequate in the face of massed Federal bayonet charges which became more common as the war progressed.

Personal equipment: Greatcoats and other heavy equipment were often abandoned in the summer without a moment's thought for the future. Great hardships resulted in the subsequent winter with several units having to be declared non-operational due to their inability to fight in the cold. The soldier here has at least retained his blanket roll and canteen.

and gaudy uniforms, although eventually even they were forced to concede the impracticality of red pantaloons and scarlet jackets in the proximity of enemy sharpshooters.

On 6 June 1861, General Order No. 4 was issued governing the distribution of the coats for officers and other ranks. Cadet gray double-breasted tunics with a long skirt extending halfway between the hip and the knee, a standing collar and twin rows of large brass buttons were introduced, but these soon fell from favor with ordinary soldiers, many of whom quickly replaced them with short-waisted single-breasted jackets requested from home. Initially officers were ordered to wear gold collar insignia – one to three gold bars (second lieutenants to captains) and one to three stars (majors to colonels) – but it was rapidly realized that, again, these made excellent targets, and on 3 June 1862, a further order was promulgated allowing officers to dispense with the insignia in the field. Self-preservation being a great spur to insubordination, there is ample evidence that many officers had unilaterally discarded their badges of rank well before

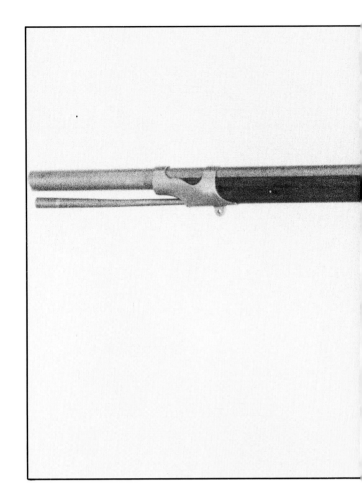

Below: Two Confederate privates pose informally for a photograph. The soldier on the left carries a Bowie knife, much favored by backwoodsmen in the early stages of the war.

then. Non-commissioned officers were issued with chevrons in branch-of-service colors but there is photographic evidence to suggest that the great majority of N.C.O.s either wore no badges of rank or introduced small, black homemade variants. As the war progressed and the effects of the blockade became more apparent, it became less possible to maintain standards in design and color so that, by late 1862, jackets were varying in hue from dark to a brownish gray and were being issued with from five to ten buttons. No longer able to control the design of their troops' uniforms, many states still attempted to preserve their local identity by issuing individually designed buttons and belt buckles, although these were not always universally available.

Waistcoats were not regulation issue. They were, however, a popular item of contemporary civilian attire and were thus often worn as supplements to the jackets, particularly in the cold winter months. Troops were issued with overcoats, but many contrived to "lose" these during the hot summer months without any thought for the future, making the waistcoat all the more important when the weather deteriorated.

Despite an undertaking given by the Confederacy as early as 19 April 1861 to provide regulation steel gray trousers for its troops, comparatively few actually seem to have been issued and most that were were sky blue. As early as the latter part of 1862, it was not uncommon to see troops in home-woven brown or butternut civilian breeches heavily patched to extract the last vestige of wear and preserve at least an element of dignity for the soldier. Typically trousers were made of wool

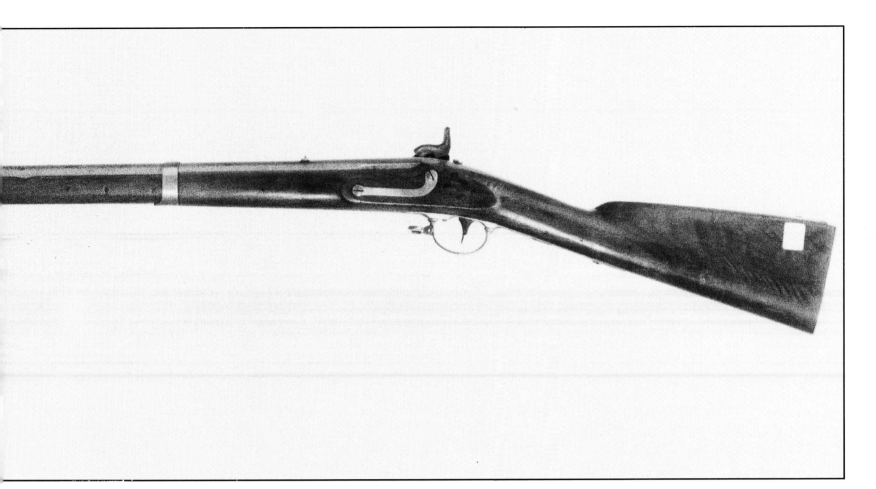

although gray denim material was common in the West. In the summer of 1862, some enterprising soldiers even resorted to the manufacture of remarkably smart (if coarse) trousers from blankets.

Shoes and boots were a constant bone of contention. At first, many volunteers provided their own heavy boots into which they tucked the tops of their trousers. After a few miles of forced marching, however, the massive high heels attached to these boots were found to be a positive liability: when the insteps wore down, the wearer was left with an uneven walking surface. Furthermore, the poor-quality leather lost all shape in the rain and actually froze solid in the winter, rendering the boots all but unwearable in inclement weather. "Jefferson" boots, either Southern-made or imported from England, were given a trial but generally proved little better than useless. Imported shoes were lined and filled with stiff paper, causing them to disintegrate in the wet, while domestically manufactured products comprised green leather which cracked in the heat. As early as the winter of 1862, frantic orders were issued to the worst-equipped troops to collect hides from the military slaughter pens for the manufacture of moccasins but, at best, this could only provide a temporary respite from a problem which was destined to plague the commissaries for the rest of the war. Many infantrymen resorted to homemade wooden clogs as the only viable alternative.

In theory, each soldier was to be issued three flannel shirts and four pairs of woolen socks, but in practice, these were often simply not available. Many issue shirts were imported and were thus in a variety of colors. Few had collars or pockets,

although certain more formal patterns were designed to be worn in lieu of uniform jackets in the summer months, particularly in the early stages of the war.

All ranks wore a variety of black or brown belts, either secured with Confederate ordnance plates depicting the letters "CSA" or with clasps of locally manufactured state design. Cartridge boxes were secured with similar plates, but these were expensive to produce and became a rarity after 1862.

Most infantrymen were issued with bayonets and scabbards of various designs, although most found them to be heavy, cumbersome, and of little use. In true Confederate tradition, many regiments discarded the weapon *en masse* without a thought for the future, although ironically a number tried to rectify this mistake once they had experienced the impact of a Union bayonet charge. Many volunteers supplemented their issue armaments with personally acquired revolvers and Bowie knives in anticipation of vicious hand-to-hand fighting, but these, too, were soon discarded as heavy and impractical as soon as the realities of actual warfare were appreciated.

By the advent of 1863, shortages were taking their toll at all levels. Troops were reduced to wearing homespun dyed civilian clothing and, in some cases, hand-me-downs. Many were forced to resort to pillaging the Federal dead and robbing prisoners, so much so that Washington felt it necessary to threaten to treat as spies Confederate soldiers captured in predominantly Union uniform: (some were actually tried and shot.) Despite this, the Army of Northern Virginia continued to function, fight, and occasionally win for two more terrible years of war.

The M-1841-pattern musket was carried by many Confederate regiments.

17

4TH ALABAMA REGIMENT

Alabama was one of the most conservative states in the deep South. The third state to secede from the Union (on 11 January 1861) its capital, Montgomery, saw the establishment of the Confederacy in February of that year and was the seat of government until its removal to its permanent base in Richmond in July.

General Orders No. 1, containing dress regulations for the newly formed "Alabama Volunteer Corps," were issued on 28 April 1861. Although there is considerable evidence that many units ignored these, the majority complied within the realms of administrative possibility. Dark blue frock coats were to be worn as were gray wool trousers and West Point-style shakos. The letters "AVC" (the "C" standing for "Corps" and not "Cadets" as has been erroneously suggested) were placed on the cap below the national eagle. Also issued were woolen overcoats of jeans material lined with heavy checked or striped osnaburg, beautifully warm in winter but heavy and totally impractical in the wet. Approximately 10,000 distinctive black felt hats with the brims looped and buttoned on the left side were ordered and became a popular item of dress when introduced.

As the "Alabama Volunteer Corps" grew and demand for uniforms began to outstrip supply, gray became the most common coat color. In August 1861, Governor Andrew Moore introduced a simpler outfit including a gray wool jacket with seven brass military buttons down the front, shoulder lapels, two belt straps, and a double, thick, standing collar lined with osnaburg. Gray trousers and a gray wool overcoat, the latter with buttons similar to those of the jacket, a detachable lined cape secured to the collar by five small brass buttons, and an adjustable waist band (a luxury for the times) completed the outfit.

By the end of 1861, the highly efficient state quartermaster's department had acquired 7,416 complete uniforms including checked or striped flannel shirts, woolen underwear, socks, gloves, shoes, and blankets. In March 1862, the central Confederate government assumed responsibility for supplying the state's troops, after which Montgomery restricted its activities to clothing reserve and militia units. Nonetheless state buttons and the ubiquitous slouch hat remained popular with volunteers, who continued to wear them long after they ceased being regulation issue.

During the same month, troops of the 1st Alabama Infantry, about to leave Montgomery to take their place in the line, were each issued with an enameled cloth knapsack, haversack, and cedar canteen. As an existing unit, they were not, however, issued with the new Confederate uniform

Porter King resigned as a judge in 1861 to take command of the Marion Light Infantry, mainly comprised of students from Howard College. The company was subsequently absorbed into the Alabama Regiment.

18

Headdress: The U.S. Military Academy-style shakos were adorned with a state eagle, a blue and white plume and the letters "AVC." By 1863 most troops had been issued with conventional Confederate gray kepis.

Frock coat: The dark blue three-quarter length frock coats with their high collars, light blue piping and ostentatious epaulettes were soon replaced by more practical gray cloth coats.

Weapons: Most Alabama Volunteers were armed as here with the M1842 smoothbore 0.69-caliber musket and M1840 model bayonet.

which was still in short supply, and they thus presented a motley impression as they marched to war, each wearing his personally supplied variant.

Due in part to the French influence from Louisiana, a number of the first volunteer units to be formed in Alabama adopted the Zouave style of uniform, although due to cost and impracticality in the field, most soon reverted to the anonymity of Confederate gray. The Alabama Zouaves (Law's Company), the Tallapoosa Zouaves (Smith's Company), and the Eufaula Zouaves (later Company "K," the 15th Alabama Infantry Regiment) were among the most famous.

The 4th Alabamans were the first troops from the state, and indeed among the first from the Confederacy, to experience formal battle. Under the command of the vastly experienced Evander Law, they were deployed as part of General Barnard Bee's Brigade when news reached General Beauregard, who was in overall command of the Confederate forces in the area, that a large Union army was approaching Manassas from the direction of Washington. Determined to hold his position until Johnston could arrive with reinforcements, Beauregard ordered Nathan Evans with the 4th South Carolina Regiment, the 1st Louisiana Special Battalion, and a squadron of cavalry to secure the river crossings, while his remaining troops, including Bee's Brigade, were ordered forward to the high ground in the vicinity of Henry House Hill, some two miles south of Bull Run. A fervent believer in taking the offensive, Evans delayed the progress of the vastly superior Federal forces for over an hour by leading a series of charges against the confused and shaken Northern ranks. Forced at last to withdraw, the remnants of Evans' troops retired to a fresh position between Bull Run and Henry House Hill where they were joined by Bee's 4th Alabamans and 2nd and 11th Mississippians and by Bartow's 7th and 8th Georgians who had force-marched to their assistance. Despite their hunger and thirst – 21 July was a blazing hot day – Bee's men were not allowed to rest but instead were deployed forward to within 100 yards (91.5m) of the enemy. Once in position, they halted and fired a series of withering volleys into the enemy lines, lying on the ground for protection against returning fire while they reloaded.

Although outnumbered three to one at 10:30 a.m., in an effort to buy yet more time until the bulk of Johnston's reinforcements could arrive, the jubilant Confederates took the initiative, rising *en masse* to charge the by now thoroughly disillusioned Northern divisions to their front. Although Bartow's Georgians on the right flank took the worst casualties (they subsequently named the area "the place of slaughter"), Bee's men suffered severely. In the words of Captain Thomas Goldsby of the 4th Alabama, "Our brave men fell in great numbers, but they died as the brave love to die – with faces to the foe, fighting in the holy cause of liberty." Whether the 30 percent casualties suffered by one Alabama company or Lieutenant Colonel Jones who died in agony, his leg shattered by enemy fire, would have agreed with those sentiments is doubtful. During the morning, every field officer of the 4th Alabama was killed or injured.

When Evans' weary men on the left and Barstow's Georgians on the right were forced to give ground, Bee found his flanks exposed and his position untenable. Forced to withdraw under heavy fire, his men now made a tragic error. Seeing a gray-clad regiment some distance off and assuming it to be part of the long-awaited reinforcements, an officer from the 4th Alabama made a recognition signal which he mistakenly thought was answered. The Alabamans moved to re-form next to the newcomers, who were in fact the gray-uniformed vanguard of Sherman's 2nd Wisconsin Regiment. Immediately the unsuspecting Southerners unfurled their colors, they were met by a murderous fire. Out of control, they abandoned their position and fled south toward Henry House Hill where the 600 South Carolinians of Hampton's Legion had formed in reserve. Eager for glory, Hampton advanced his troops toward the enemy and, for a while, found himself all alone and in the forefront of the battle. Within minutes, the South Carolinians were cut to pieces and forced to join the general retreat.

Meanwhile the Confederate rear had been reinforced by Jackson's five regiments of Virginia infantry. Despite strong protestations from Bee, Jackson refused to advance his troops in support of the shattered front-line brigades, although he did order his artillery to fire into the advancing Federals. Exasperated, Bee turned, rallied the exhausted remnants of the 4th Alabamans, and led them back over the crest of Henry House Hill toward the enemy. It was a gallant but hopeless effort. The Union artillery battered the Alabamans so badly that, once again, they broke and ran. In a desperate attempt to hold his command together, Bee turned and charged the enemy. A few seconds later, he was shot off his horse, mortally wounded. Exhausted but unbowed, the few remaining Alabamans re-formed around their regimental banner and, under the command of a color sergeant, were at last able to take up a position in reserve on the right of the now heavily reinforced Confederate line.

Evander Law, the lieutenant colonel of the 4th Alabama at 1st Manassas, was severely wounded during the fighting. Fully recovered, he was elected colonel on 8 October 1861 and given command of Whiting's Brigade, which included his old regiment. Having led the brigade during the Peninsula campaign and at Malvern Hill, 2nd Manassas, and Antietam (Sharpsburg), he was promoted brigadier general on 3 October 1862. He led his brigade in the attack on the Round Tops during the Battle of Gettysburg, assuming command of the division when Hood was wounded. He again succeeded Hood at Chickamauga but reverted to brigade command during the Wilderness campaign and at Spotsylvania, North Anna, and Cold Harbor where he was again badly wounded. Sent to the Carolinas to recuperate, he assumed command of Butler's cavalry brigade in February 1865.

After Law's injury at Cold Harbor in June 1864, control of his old brigade, which then constituted the 4th, 15th, 44th, 47th, and 48th Alabama Regiments, passed to Brigadier General Perry who retained command until the final surrender.

A memorial to the Canebrake Rifles, later to become Company 'B' of the 4th Alabama Regiment.

THE CONFEDERATE IRREGULAR

As the war progressed and the Federal blockade tightened, many Confederate troops were, of necessity, forced to wear irregular items of clothing. The lucky ones – the so-called "Butternuts" – were issued with apparel made from cheap, mass-produced, coarse gray cloth which at least resembled uniform. The less fortunate were compelled to supplement their existing uniforms with captured or looted items of Union kit. Most confined their pillaging to anonymous items of clothing such as shirts, underwear, socks and shoes, although articles such as overcoats and raincoats and even jackets and trousers were widely worn. Where possible, the strictly military items of kit were dyed gray or butternut.

The acquisition and use by the Confederates of essential clothing items was accepted by the Federals as inevitable and justifiable. However, the wearing of their uniforms by spies and pro-Confederate guerrillas was not tolerated.

Matters came to a head in 1863 when the tide of battle began to turn convincingly against the South. On 26 January, General Grant, in command of the Department of the Tennessee, ordered that: "guerrillas or Southern soldiers caught in the uniforms of Federal soldiers would not be treated as organized bodies of the enemy but would be closely confined and held for the action of the War Depart-

Union troops recapturing a wagon train from a group of Confederate guerrillas in Virginia, September 1863.

ment. Those caught within the lines of the Federal army in such uniforms or in civilian clothing would be treated as spies."

On 29 March, the commander of the Department of Maryland went further, formally ordering that any officer or soldier of the Confederate army found within Federal lines wearing clothing or accouterments of the United States would be dealt with as a spy. The Southern authorities threatened retaliation, arguing that such clothing and accouterments were legitimate bounty under the rules of war and might therefore be worn by the capturing forces. In an attempt to defuse the volatile situation, Adjutant General Francis Lieber issued a series of general orders expounding clearly Washington's attitude toward enemy troops captured in Federal uniform. General Order No. 100, dated 24 April 1863, stated:

Troops who fight in the uniform of their enemies, without any plain, striking, and uniform mark of distinction of their own, can expect no quarter. If American troops capture a train containing uniforms of the enemy, and the commander considers it advisable to distribute them for use among his men, some striking mark or sign must be adopted to distinguish the American soldier from the enemy.

After 1863 resupply became increasingly difficult for the Confederate forces. Many troops resorted to civilian homespun while others supplemented their uniform from items of kit looted from prisoners and the dead. A few irregulars fought unashamedly for plunder. Though subject to summary execution if caught, they frequently resorted to Federal uniform to gain the element of surprise. Although their greatest excesses were disowned by the Confederacy many, notably William Quantrill, held Southern commissions.

Lieber's well-considered statement had little immediate effect on the Confederates. Only four days later, the commander of the 8th Missouri Cavalry reported the murder of seven of his men by "rebels dressed in Federal Uniform who rode up to them as friends," stripped and murdered them and then, as a final insult, threw them into a heap "like so many hogs."

On 30 August 1863, Sherman complained to Grant that his troops had recently captured two men professing to belong to the Confederate cavalry. Neither wore uniform nor indeed anything to suggest the mark of a soldier, although both were fully armed and had taken active steps to avoid the Northern patrols. The fate of these men is unknown, although others like them met unfortunate ends. Private Dodd of the 8th Texas Cavalry was shot as a spy on 5 January 1864 when caught wearing United States uniform, and three days

later, the Department of Ohio issued an order directing corps commanders to execute by firing squad any Confederate soldier caught wearing Federal uniform within Union lines. However, despite the obviously strong feeling of the commanders on the ground, Washington showed a marked reluctance to support such strong measures. In several instances, field orders that sentenced to death "spies" in hybrid uniform were revoked.

Not surprisingly, the government was far less compromising in its attitude toward the bushwacker. Vicious, blood-thirsty, and self-centered, the bushwacker, or raider, fought far more for himself than he did for the Confederacy, although a number were awarded protective commissions in the Southern army. Prevalent in the border states, particularly Missouri and what was to become West Virginia, he was detested by most and feared by all. Captain Charles Leib, an officer in the Union army, described a group of raiders whom he encountered in western Virginia:

> Imagine a stolid, vicious-looking countenance, an ungainly figure [clothed] in a garb of the coarsest texture of homespun linen or linsey-woolsey, tattered and torn, and so covered with dirt as not to enable one to guess its original color; a dilapidated, rimless hat or cap of some wild animal covering his head, which has not been combed for months; his feet covered with moccasins, and a rifle by his side, a powder horn and a shot-pouch slung around his neck ... Thus equipped, he sallies forth with the stealth of a panther, and lies in wait for a straggling soldier ... to whom the only warning given of his presence is the sharp click of his deadly weapon.

The most notorious raider, William Clarke Quantrill, was not even a Southerner. The son of an Ohio schoolteacher, he had drifted around the West until the advent of the war had given him the opportunity to practice his particular talents. Despite his lack of Confederate ties, he chose to support the cause of the South because of the potential afforded him to attack the symbols of Missouri authority which he had grown to detest.

Quantrill gathered about him a gang of psychopathic killers, including four men who were later destined to become infamous in their own right: Frank and Jessie James, and Cole and James Younger. Initially theirs was a relatively conventional war in which Union supply lines and bases were attacked in conjunction with more orthodox Confederate military operations. In August 1862, Quantrill's band captured Independence, Missouri as part of a Southern cavalry raid against Arkansas, and as a reward, Quantrill received a captain's commission in the Confederate army. Thereafter he referred to himself as "Colonel" as if to imply the respectability of regimental status for his group.

Quantrill was totally unscrupulous. Capable of double crossing his own men, of murder in cold blood, and of every type of subterfuge, he insured that his men were well mounted and armed by stealing from enemy and neutral alike. On one occasion, he pretended to support a pro-abolitionist attack aimed at freeing slaves while, at the same time, fore-

Confederate irregulars rarely if ever wore a uniform and therefore could expect little quarter if captured. Denied an amnesty after the war, many turned to crime as a way of life.

warning the plantation owner of the raid. The attackers were massacred, leaving Quantrill and his gang free to plunder their dead bodies.

Quantrill's most blood-chilling raid began before dawn on 21 August 1863 when, with about 450 men, he attacked and sacked the town of Lawrence, Kansas, a center for abolitionism and therefore a special target for the Confederates. At the time of the raid, the guerrillas were in a highly vengeful mood. In an attempt to prevent the outlaws' wives and sisters feeding and sheltering their kinfolk, Thomas Ewing, the local Union commander, had ordered the arrest all adult female relatives and their transportation under guard to Kansas City. There, on 14 August, a building housing many of the women collapsed, burying five of them beneath the rubble.

The carnage began immediately the band crossed the Kansas border. Ten farmers were kidnapped to guide the guerrillas toward unsuspecting Lawrence; they were murdered, one by one, as soon as their usefulness was over. Quantrill's only order to his followers was to "kill every male and burn every house" – instructions which they carried out with alacrity. The first of the Lawrence residents to die was a United Brethren clergyman shot through the head while milking his cow. During the next three hours, 182 men and boys were murdered, many in full view of their mothers, wives, and children, and 185 buildings destroyed. At about nine o'clock in the morning, a column of advancing Union cavalry was spotted by a lookout, and the gang made good its escape without sustaining a single injury.

Only the most partisan were unmoved by this shocking occurrence. A manhunt for Quantrill's followers netted a number who were summarily hanged or shot, but most escaped into the Missouri backwoods. General Ewing ordered the forcible removal of over 10,000 civilians from the four Missouri counties bordering Kansas and declared the area a war zone in the hope of cutting off the guerrillas from their supplies.

In October 1863, while on their way to Texas and winter quarters, Quantrill and his men, dressed in stolen Union uniforms, met a group of Federal troops en route for Fort Baxter Springs, Kansas. Taking the Northerners by surprise (they had assumed that Quantrill and his men were a welcoming party), the guerrillas slaughtered without mercy the majority of the young, unsuspecting soldiers.

The trail of murder and carnage continued until May 1865 when the 27-year-old Quantrill was surprised by Union troops in Kentucky and mortally wounded. When he died a month later, few mourned his passing.

John Morgan's "highwaymen" were notorious. Here they are shown sacking a peaceful town in the west.

THE CONFEDERATE ENGINEER

From the point of view of engineering, the Confederacy began the Civil War at a distinct disadvantage. The vast majority of the officers and men comprising the small but efficient regular army Corps of Engineers and Corps of Topographical Engineers elected to remain loyal to the Union, leaving the South without a nucleus of professional experience on which to build. The Confederacy did, however, have two saving graces: her comparative lack of size and the unswerving support of Robert E. Lee, himself a military engineer of some stature. With the exception of the ill-fated Gettysburg campaign, Confederate armies were never called on to advance deep into enemy territory or to sustain themselves far from the presence of sympathetic civilians, and therefore they never experienced the very real problem of maintaining long lines of supply and communication. They had to repair rather than build bridges and military highways, and were able to rely on an existing (if small) network of railroads for communication. Unlike the Northern railroads which were largely dependent on coal, most Southern locomotives were wood burners and, as such, were far easier to provision.

As early as 1860, Virginia formed its own state Corps of Engineers from the few professional engineers available, utilizing their skills in the construction of a line of coastal and frontier forts. Initially, this unit remained independent, dressing in the standard U.S. officers' dark blue uniform with white belt, gold badges of rank, and state buttons and cap badges according to the Virginia dress regulations of 2 March 1858. However, when the Confederate government moved to Richmond the following year, this small cadre, which consisted totally of officers, merged into the Confederate Corps of Engineers.

Initially, the Corps remained small and exclusive. The actual construction of fortifications, roads, and bridges was undertaken by unskilled labor drawn from available infantry units placed under the temporary command of engineering officers or civilian sub-contractors employed for specific tasks. During the Peninsula campaign (March – July 1862), the system was regulated somewhat, and in June of that year, the Chief of Engineers of the Army of Northern Virginia was directed to take 300 men from each division to form a Corps of Pioneers

Confederate defenses, such as these at Fort Sedgewick, did much to frustrate the Northern streamroller and to prolong the war.

Headdress: Initially officers were instructed to wear "fore and aft" staff officers' hats. However as the war progressed they tended to wear whatever they could find. Cap badges comprising a pair of silver-plated crossed flags were occasionally issued.

Tunic: The staff officer's uniform with buff facings and red sashes, which officially constituted an Engineer Officer's dress, was rarely worn. Instead most favored gray or brown jackets with matching trousers. A variety of infantry-pattern swords, pistols and carbines were carried for personal protection.

27

to work under the direct control of the engineers. Despite the bravery and diligence of the Pioneer Corps, there were too few of them and they were too lacking in skill to be truly effective. On occasion, they were simply not available, in which case the engineer in charge of a project was entitled to use his initiative and resort to available resources. In one instance, an officer, tasked with bridging the James River near Richmond and finding that the Pioneers had been deployed elsewhere, had 500 civilians rounded up by the Provost Marshal and marched under guard to do the job.

In late 1863, as the battered remnants of the Army of Northern Virginia retreated south into the Virginia hinterland, the necessity for a regularly constituted Corps of Engineers comprising enlisted men as well as officers was at last conceded. Two regiments – the 1st and 2nd Regiments of Confederate States Engineers, each consisting of ten companies of 100 men – were authorized by the Confederate Congress and formed in time for the intended 1864 offensive. The 1st Regiment and two companies of the 2nd served with the Army of Northern Virginia, while the remainder were posted to the West.

Initially, few staff officers fully understood the potential of the new Corps, so much so that much of the 1st Regiment spent its initial engagement fighting as infantry, a duty which it performed more than adequately. However, as the war continued and the need for punitive, slowing action became more apparent, the engineers became more accepted in their true role of building fortifications and defending them with equal ease and ability. As the retreat to Appomattox progressed, engineer elements were constantly to be found at the head of the army, building bridges to facilitate its continued withdrawal, while their colleagues brought up the rear and held off the enemy by destroying the same bridges once their usefulness had been served.

Inevitably, skill comes with age, and because of this, the Corps of Engineers did not consist of young men. Most were between the ages of 25 and 35 and married, and were skilled artisans in their own right. Field and company officers were engineers by profession in civilian life, as were many of the junior officers.

Officers of the Corps of Engineers wore regulation staff officers' uniforms with buff facings, red sashes, and (when available) buttons depicting the Old English letter "E." However, during the latter stages of the war when uniform became difficult if not impossible to acquire, most resorted to conventional officer attire supplemented where necessary by civilian clothing. Enlisted men did not have an authorized button but instead wore general service ones and, toward the end, even plain wooden buttons. Typically, they wore waist-length gray or brown jackets with matching trousers, brown boots and belts, gray regulation kepis, cloth haversacks, and water canteens. Non-commissioned officers wore either buff or white chevrons and, in more established posts, a white cotton stripe down each leg. In keeping with their dual role as artisans and infanteers, most engineers carried rifles and ammunition pouches as well as the ubiquitous shovels.

The massive fortifications built for the defense of Petersburg and Richmond owed much to the inspirational genius of General Lee, himself an accomplished engineer. Built in 1862 and regularly strengthened thereafter, they withstood the concerted might of the Army of the Potomac during the final stages of the war and might well have enabled the garrisons of both cities to continue their resistance almost indefinitely had Lee not been forced to withdraw the bulk of his troops westward in a final desperate attempt to avert defeat. As it was, Petersburg held out until 2 April 1865 while Richmond was abandoned, rather than fell, to the enemy.

Immediately on taking overall command in 1862, Lee had ordered the creation of a network of defensive lines around Richmond. Each divisional commander was allocated a sector and ordered to

Confederate fortifications at Vicksburg, although largely built by unskilled labor, were brilliantly conceived and in many instances bore the hallmark of Robert E. Lee himself.

construct defenses along its length utilizing all raw material available. Initially, these defenses comprised a confused mixture of trenches interspersed with areas of wooden revetments, but as the months went by, the line was developed into a complex arrangement of fire steps, artillery positions, and support trenches as sophisticated as any constructed during World War I.

More worldly wise than their Union foes, Confederate soldiers quickly became skillful in the construction of impromptu defensive trenches. Within an hour of halting – and without goading – regiments would construct shelters made of fences, stones, and logs supplemented by earth and sods, which were proof against all but artillery. They would dig full rifle pits in a day and parapets with fire steps and shelters within two. With the help of trained engineers, these localized defenses were often turned into veritable fortresses to the extent that, during the last few months of the war, seven out of eight Union frontal assaults failed despite the North's overwhelming superiority in numbers and firepower.

The Confederate States Corps of Engineers fought its greatest battle at a time when defeat was imminent. Between 29 March and the final Confederate surrender at Appomattox on 9 April 1865, the remnants of the Army of Northern Virginia fought desperately in an attempt to link up with Johnston's forces retreating from Sherman in North Carolina. Harried by Sheridan's cavalry and pursued relentlessly by Grant's overwhelming forces, the hard-pressed, starving, and exhausted Southerners fought a series of desperate rearguard actions in an attempt to buy time. While the cavalry stood and fought at Namozine Church (3 April) and Amelia Courthouse (5 April), the rest of Lee's forces retreated north, crossing the Appomattox River. During the last few hours of the war, the engineers desperately supported Ewell's infantry at Sayler's Creek and High Bridge (6 April) and at Farmville (7 April). Bridges were blown and obstacles built but to no avail. After the brief but bloody engagements at Appomattox Station (8 April) and Appomattox Courthouse on the following day, Lee sought unconditional surrender. Exact losses during this final campaign are unclear due to the large number of desertions. What is certain is that, to the bitter end, no corps served the cause of the Confederacy more ably than its Corps of Engineers.

The task of the engineer was as much to rebuild as to destroy. It became the common practice of all armies to retreat to lay waste the communications around them without giving much thought to the possibilities of counterattack.

THE CONFEDERATE BUTTERNUT

Few of those who advocated secession at any price in the heady days of 1860 had any real conception of total war. Many accepted that Washington would fight for the restoration of the status quo, but the overriding feeling was that the Federal government would agree to an equitable compromise after a limited period of saber-rattling. Total warfare encompassing entire communities – male and female, combatant and civilian – was simply beyond the comprehension of even the greatest pessimist. When war broke out a year later, early Confederate victories shrouded the reality of the growing casualty lists and the inevitability of a Union victory. The battles of Seven Pines (Fair Oaks) and the Seven Days fought in May and June 1862 within a few miles of Richmond shocked the final residue of the complacent South to the core, but by then it was too late. The United States – North and South – was experiencing absolute warfare, and the Confederacy was fighting for its very existence.

The South was never able to clothe or provision its mushrooming army adequately. Although it controlled the cotton plantations, the mills were either under Union control or across a hostile ocean patrolled by a powerful blockading fleet. Furthermore it needed to export its entire cotton harvest throughout the war simply to pay for essential arms and ammunition.

Initially most troops were clothed and equipped by the individual states, relieving the central government of the responsibility. However, as the various units were gradually merged into a single army, it became increasingly clear that there would simply not be enough official pattern gray uniforms to go around. This problem was compounded by the total inability of the average Southern soldier to look after what little he had. From the outset, discipline within the Confederate army was appalling. Of proven excellence in battle, the Southern troops, particularly the cavalry, saw little reason to be regimental at other times. Officers were voted into their commands rather than appointed on merit, and as a result, they rarely risked crossing their subordinates by inflicting what they as well as their men saw as tiresome irrelevancies. When an item of equipment, however valuable or scarce, became momentarily useless, it was treated as an impediment and discarded even though its presence might be crucial in the future. Cold weather gear was abandoned *en masse* with the coming of hot weather in the summer of 1862 as if to negate the ferocity of the winter that would inevitably follow.

Such a grave irresponsibility on the men's part had ramifications well above regimental level, never more so than during the Mine Run campaign (November–December 1863). Meade, with the Army

Confederate troops pose for an impromptu photograph at a base camp in Warrington Navy Yard, Pensacola, Florida, in 1861. The lack of formal uniform is all too apparent.

Headdress: Felt hats, gray or blue kepis, anything which would offer protection from the elements, were pressed into action.

Jackets: Uniformity was virtually non-existent. Original uniforms were merged with looted Federal gear and civilian clothing to offer a modicum of decency. Outfits were coarse, patched and ragged. Those without boots simply tucked their trousers into their socks.

Equipment: Personal effects were reduced to a minimum, all surplus articles being discarded. Most troops carried a haversack, canteen and tin mug but little else. Even cartridge pouches were abandoned, it being considered easier to carry ammunition loose in the pockets.

of the Potomac, had earlier taken the initiative and attempted to maneuver Lee out of his strong position on the Rapidan River. He executed a successful crossing with five corps at Germanna Ford and then turned west toward Orange Courthouse. Lee's cavalry, skirmishing far ahead of his lines, detected the movement immediately, allowing the Confederate Army of Northern Virginia plenty of time to dig in along strong points in the Mine Run area. Finding no obvious weaknesses in the enemy position, Meade ordered a general withdrawal without a fight and went into winter quarters around Culpeper. Sensing the confusion and indecision in the Federal command, Lee at once ordered a general advance behind Northern lines, only to be told that his men had thrown away their overcoats and could not therefore operate in the harsh winter cold beyond the protective mantle of their base camp, with its hot food and fires.

Clothes that were issued were rarely properly cared for – once again demonstrating the inability of company officers to instil minimum standards of appearance. Soap had become a sought-after luxury by 1862, with the result that little if any was squandered on the washing of clothes. Shirts, socks, and undergarments became vermin infested for the want of a hot scrub. Comparatively new clothes were frequently abandoned as unwearable even though a soaking in boiling water would have restored them to near-pristine condition. Strangely, even when the Confederates were fighting close to their own cities, matters did not improve, there being no obvious attempts made by the civilian authorities to set up improvised central laundries.

The Confederate soldier's tenacity, independence, and unshakeable belief in his cause were his greatest assets yet, at the same time, his greatest enemies. Proud of their reputation as hard fighters and never men prone to inquiring too far into the future, the Confederates simply did not see the need for discipline. As long as they kept their weapons clean and their powder dry and turned up when and where their presence was required, what did it matter how they got there or what they looked like? There were, of course, exceptions to this generalization. "Stonewall" Jackson commanded the finest light infantry in the world during the campaigns of 1862–63, but he would not have been able to execute the complex and lengthy maneuvers that he did without a strong sense of motivation assisted by excellent discipline. Even so, his troops were often likened to scarecrows and tramps as they appeared suddenly and unexpectedly behind enemy lines.

Kit replacement became a near impossibility from late 1862 onward. Many Confederate troops

The Confederate charge on Missionary Ridge during the Battle of Chattanooga. Sheer determination did much to overcome the chronic lack of supplies.

relied upon Federal equipment pilfered from prisoners or the dead to augment their own meager issue, but this became unpopular when rumors began to spread that the North was treating Southerners caught in Union uniform behind its lines as spies. Many families attempted to send what they could from home, but inevitably, clothing provided domestically was civilian in nature and left the soldiers resembling armed farm boys rather than soldiers.

The most realistic solution lay in the wholesale issue of a new homespun uniform made of cheap, durable cloth. Never popular with the Confederate authorities, who perpetually strove to establish at least some degree of formality within their forces, the new issue was intended to supplement rather than replace the traditional gray. Nevertheless by 1865, few units were wearing anything but the new issue.

The new uniform quickly attained the universally accepted nickname "butternut" after a group of farmers from Ohio, Indiana, and Illinois who had thrown in their lot with the Confederacy. Violently anti-"Yankee," these smallholders had, during the previous 50 years, evolved a corn–hog–whiskey economy in the rural south of that region. Totally divorced from the more affluent settlers of New England heritage who farmed to the north, theirs was a totally isolated society. They dressed in homespun clothes dyed with the oil of walnut or butternut trees, and hence acquired the generic name "Butternuts."

Butternut first appeared extensively at South Mountain (14 September 1862), when it was noticed that hundreds of the Confederate dead were wearing the new, coarse uniform. Production was simple and ideally suited the home economy then being forced by necessity on the South. Wool and cotton were carded together and spun into yarn. This was then dyed with walnut or butternut oil and woven into cloth on homemade looms. The cloth was then dyed again until it became a reddish brown, after which it was cut and sewn into uniforms.

Any carpenter could make a loom and any woman could operate it. As the Northern soldiers marched deeper into the South, they were amazed to see the extent of manufacture of butternut. Many houses had improvised looms, and those that did not invariably had the means to card the wool and cotton, and spinning wheels to turn them into yarn.

Always short of clothing and equipment, the Southern soldier was in many ways the author of his own discomfort. Nevertheless had it not been for the resilience and productivity of his womenfolk at home, he might well have been in a far worse predicament.

The charge of the 6th Missouri Regiment at Vicksburg. The lack of formal uniforms did nothing to reduce the fighting potency of these gallant men.

THE VIRGINIA CAVALRY

The "Black Horse Cavalry," as it was known, did much to snatch victory from defeat at Manassas on 21 July 1861 when they held, and eventually routed, the New York Fire Zouaves.

Not the first state to secede from the Union, Virginia was nonetheless politically and economically the most powerful in the Confederacy. It contained the Confederate capital, several strategically important ports, many of the railheads, and much of the South's industrial output. Its greatest weakness lay in its geographical position as a border state, a problem which was severely compounded when the disenchanted pro-abolitionist mining communities across the Blue Ridge Mountains voted to form the independent state of West Virginia and return to the Union in 1863. Virginia's main rail link with the west passed through Manassas Junction which was relatively close to the Maryland border and less than 40 miles from the outskirts of Washington. More crucially, the northern part of the Shenandoah Valley – the aptly named "breadbasket of the Confederacy" – lay dangerously exposed to marauding Federal cavalry parties.

During the early stages of the war when the Confederacy was in the ascendancy, none of this mattered. Two battles fought for the control of Manassas Junction – the 1st and 2nd Battles of Manassas (Bull Run) – both ended in comprehensive Southern victories, and by early 1862, it was Washington rather than Richmond which faced the possibility of capitulation. However, as the war progressed and the sheer industrial might of the North began to take its inevitable toll, the situation began slowly but steadily to change. In early 1864, the Shenandoah Valley was comprehensively sacked by vengeful Union troops, and from then until the final Confederate surrender, Virginia was destined to suffer severely at the hands of an increasingly uncompromising enemy.

With the exception of western Virginia, which provided no fewer than 12,688 volunteers to the Union cause in 1861 alone, large numbers of men from all parts of Virginia flocked to enlist in the Confederate army. Initially organization and training of the state troops were delegated to an erratic and somewhat eccentric professor from the Virginia Military Institute, but in mid-May control passed to General Joseph Johnston. A West Point graduate, a veteran of the Seminole and Mexican wars and a trusted friend of Robert E. Lee, Johnston assumed command of all facets of training in the South once the Virginian forces were absorbed into the Confederate army.

Initially Johnston's Army of the Shenandoah consisted of 10,000 officers and enlisted men organized into four brigades, each with its own artillery battery but all sharing the services of the 1st Virginia Cavalry under the command of Colonel

Headdress: Many Virginians adorned their irregular slouch hats with feathers as if to emphasize their éliteness.

Jackets: Jackets of all kinds were worn with or without regulation Confederate collar and cuffs. Officers wore badges of rank on their shoulders and sleeves, N.C.O.s on their upper arm.

Firearms: Issue sabers were soon abandoned as impractical. Troops were given pistols but usually supplemented the firepower of these with privately purchased carbines and even in a few instances with shotguns.

35

Jeb Stuart. As the army grew and the cavalry expanded, the latter was re-formed into an independent brigade, but it never really lost its strong Virginia bias.

When first established, the 1st Virginia Cavalry (or "Black Horse Cavalry" as it was locally known) consisted of four troops of 100 men each, but by the summer of 1861, it had grown to a full regiment of ten troops. Its members regarded themselves as a social and military élite. All were accomplished horsemen used to hard riding and most were excellent shots. The regiment served with the Army of Northern Virginia throughout the war, performing invaluable reconaissance duty as well as undertaking several daring raids deep behind enemy territory. It was present at the 1st and 2nd Battles of Manassas, at Fredericksburg and Chancellorsville, and at the great cavalry action at Brandy Station. After Stuart's death at Yellow Tavern, the regiment continued in service, finishing the war as part of Munford's Brigade.

At no time did the 1st Virginians show their true worth more than during the 1st Battle of Manassas when the presence of these superb horsemen did much to turn defeat into victory. The rebel line was being hard pressed when Stuart and his regiment arrived from the south to take up a position on the extreme Confederate left flank below Henry House Hill. Well deployed in a patch of woods, the Virginians managed to keep their presence concealed from the Union troops until the latter had been committed to a frontal assault up the hill against what they assumed to be the remnants of the rapidly disintegrating Southern army. In a spirited charge, a squadron of Stuart's 1st Virginians tore into the unsuspecting lines of the 11th New York Fire Zouaves, leaving the latter, and with them the entire Union right flank, shaken and demoralized. The Union assault quickly wavered and, within minutes, disintegrated into a general withdrawal. Panic set in among the raw Union troops, turning an orderly retreat into a full-scale rout. The Confederate cavalry was not disciplined enough to pursue the enemy and were thus unable to exploit their victory to the full. Nonetheless, in two hours of bloody fighting the Virginian cavalry earned for itself a reputation for invulnerability which it was to retain at least until Brandy Station.

Members of the 1st Virginian wore gray or butternut uniform adorned with numerous troop and personal variations. Many troopers sported long, flowing hair despite its impracticality in the field.

Others wore often ornate plumes and feathers in their non-regulation slouch hats. Shell jackets, double-breasted fatigue blouses, and Federal-style fatigue dress, with or without the regulation Confederate yellow collar and cuffs, were all worn. Where possible, officers retained the elaborate cuff braiding, or "chicken guts," on their long frock coats or shell jackets. Commissioned rank was indicated both by insignia worn on the collar and by the design of the sleeve braiding: lieutenants, captains, field officers, and generals wore from one to four strands respectively. N.C.O.s wore yellow chevrons and $1\frac{3}{4}$-inch (4.5cm) stripes on the outer seams of their light blue trousers. Theoretically senior N.C.O.s also wore distinctive yellow sashes, but these were regarded as both an unnecessary encumbrance and an invitation to enemy sharpshooters and were invariably discarded.

A wide variety of high boots were worn, usually over but occasionally under the light blue or gray corduroy trousers. The black leather belt with its pistol holster and ammunition pouch was fastened with a circular Virginia state buckle.

The Virginians were among the first cavalry troops to abandon the saber, although whether this was due more to its impracticality or to its rarity is a moot point. Carbines and pistols of every kind were provided by the individual troopers and carried into battle. Although this ameliorated considerably the initial problems of supply, ultimately it made ammunition replenishment a logistical nightmare. In the absence of carbines, sawn-off, double-barreled, muzzle-loading shotguns were found to be most effective, although the indiscriminate discharge of such weapons by excited troops in the heat of battle did tend to endanger both friend and foe alike.

As the war progressed, Virginia continued to provide the bulk of the Confederate cavalry. In August 1864, Fitzhugh Lee's entire division consisted of seven Virginian regiments, the 1st to 4th of which formed a veteran brigade under the irrepressible Brigadier General W.C. Wickham. Wickham was typical of the cavalry leaders of the time. A graduate of the University of Virginia, he devoted his pre-war energies to his legal practice and to the running of the family plantation. Although opposed to secession, he volunteered and fought for the Confederacy at the 1st Battle of Manassas during which he served as a captain in the élite Hanover Dragoons. Promoted lieutenant colonel and placed in command of the 4th Virginia Cavalry

The Tallassee carbine was used extensively throughout the Confederate States army.

36

in September 1861, he was severely wounded by a saber thrust in hand-to-hand fighting during the Battle of Williamsburg (4–5th May 1862). While convalescing at home, he was captured by McClellan but subsequently exchanged for his wife's relative, Thomas Kane of the Pennsylvania Bucktails. Restored to command of the 4th Virginia and promoted colonel in August 1862, he led his regiment at the 2nd Battle of Manassas, at Boonsborough, at Antietam (Sharpsburg), and on Stuart's raid into Maryland and Pennsylvania. Wounded while in temporary command of Fitzhugh Lee's Brigade at Upperville, Wickham recovered in time to lead his men at Fredericksburg, Chancellorsville, and Gettysburg. Appointed brigadier general on 1 September 1863, he served under

Fitzhugh Lee in the Mine Run operations, at Brandy Station, and at Buckland Mills before repelling Kilpatrick's raid on Richmond in February 1864. Thereafter he commanded his unit during the Wilderness campaign, at Spotsylvania and Yellow Tavern, and during a number of minor engagements, before retiring to take up his seat in the Confederate Congress on 9 November 1864.

By April 1865, Fitzhugh Lee's Division consisted almost exclusively of Virginians. Munford's Brigade, the successor to Wickham's Brigade, contained the 1st to 4th Virginians, Payne's Brigade comprised the 5th, 6th, 8th, and 36th Virginians, while Gary's somewhat assorted unit contained the 24th Regiment. No state could have given more to its beloved Confederacy.

To many Virginians, John Brown's stand at Harpers Ferry proved the inevitability of war and hastened the break-up of the Union.

HOOD'S TEXAS BRIGADE

The Lone Star State of Texas seceded on 1 February 1861, less than 15 years after being admitted to the Union. The governor, Sam Houston was firmly against the split but was forced to concede when a state convention voted by 166 to 8 to throw in their lot with the South.

Texas did not immediately call for volunteers but instead decided to bide its time and await events. Impatient for action and despairing of the state government's inactivity, many Texans moved east to offer their services to the newly formed Confederate army. Several infantry units were formed, and on 12 November 1861, the 3rd and 5th Texas Infantry Regiments, under the commands of John B. Hood and J.J. Archer respectively, linked with the 18th Georgia under W.T. Wofford to form the Texas Brigade. Overall command initially passed to Colonel Lewis T. Wigfall of the 1st Texas Infantry, but when he was elected to the Confederate Senate, his place was taken by the newly promoted Brigadier General Hood.

A blond giant with doleful eyes and a quiet, unassuming manner, John Bell Hood was without peer as a brigade or divisional leader, at which level he was able to subordinate his lack of basic intelligence to his sheer charisma and will to win. In less than six months, he turned his brigade into, in the words of Lee, "the best combat troops in the Army

of Northern Virginia." When Hood was promoted major general and posted to command of the 2nd Division on 10 October 1862, the Texans paid him the highest compliment possible by retaining his name as part of the brigade title. From then to its disbandment at the very end of the war, it remained "Hood's Texas Brigade."

Under Hood's inspired leadership, the brigade was blooded at Gaines's Mill (27 June 1862) after which its numbers were supplemented by the addition of Colonel M. Gary's Hampton Legion. Despite its somewhat grandiose title, the Legion in fact consisted of six companies of South Carolina infantrymen formed, paid for, and maintained (together with four cavalry companies and a battery of artillery) by the immensely wealthy Wade Hampton. The entire Legion was led by the inexperienced Hampton at the 1st Battle of Manassas (Bull Run) during which it fought with distinction but sustained 20 percent casualties. Thereafter it was broken up, the artillery being redesignated Hart's South Carolina Battery, the cavalry joining Rosser's cavalry regiment, and the infantry joining Hood.

Prior to relinquishing command to Colonel Jerome Bonaparte Robertson of the 5th Texan Infantry, Hood again led his brigade during the 2nd Battle of Manassas and at Antietam (Sharpsburg).

Longstreet's Texans retaking the outer line of entrenchments on the south side of the James River.

Headdress: Officially the Texas Brigade wore Federal pattern kepis. However as the war progressed many abandoned these in favor of slouch hats often adorned with a feather. As if to emphasize Texan independence, troops of all ranks tended to favor the Lone Star hat badge, although the trooper here has retained the more orthodox crossed sabers.

Jacket: Many of the first companies formed adopted styles and patterns later associated with neighboring states. In this instance the trooper is wearing a Mississippi-style jacket with high collar and several rows of stripes across the chest.

During the later stages of 1862, the brigade was restructured to return it to full strength, the 1st, 4th, and 5th Texan Regiments being joined by the 3rd Arkansas under the command of Colonel Van Manning.

When Robertson received his third wound during the Battle of Gettysburg, when the Texans fought as part of Hood's Division, he was temporarily replaced by Colonel P. Work. Reinstated when the brigade moved to the West, Robertson led his men into action at Chickamauga (19–20 September 1863), but by then he had lost the support of General Longstreet. When Jenkins replaced Hood as divisional commander, Robertson lost his one remaining ally and was removed from command, his place being taken by the Texan John Gregg. Returning to the East, the brigade once again distinguished itself during the Wilderness campaign, during which, on 6 May 1864, it lost over 400 men out of 711 in action during a single unsupported attack.

Lieutenant General John B. Hood, after whom the famous Texas Brigade was named.

Gregg was killed on 7 October 1864 during the Petersburg campaign, after which command passed in quick succession to Colonels Winkler, Bass and Powell, the latter holding the position until the final surrender.

At no time did Hood's Texan Brigade conduct itself more bravely than during the three days of bitter fighting at Gettysburg (1–3 July 1863). Realizing that the Confederacy could not hope to win a protracted war, Lee had advanced deep into Federal territory to draw Meade's Army of the Potomac away from Virginia. Gambling on the belief that a Southern victory on Northern soil would strengthen the growing peace movement in the North and

Oates with 500 men from the 15th and 47th Alabama successfully took the Devil's Den with few losses. However, fate now turned against the Confederacy. During the few minutes which Oates allowed his men to draw breath before turning north to cross the saddle separating them from Little Round Top, the Federals brought forward reserves, including Battery "D" of the 5th U.S. Artillery, pre-empting a further Confederate advance with considerable loss of life. During a confused afternoon of gallant fighting, the Southern brigades mounted a series of costly individual assaults against the by now heavily defended Federal positions on Little Round Top.

Privately-purchased hunting rifles with reinforced barrels and crude sights were carried by marksmen of both armies.

might encourage Britain's intervention on behalf of the South, Lee began the movement of his troops north from Chancellorsville on 3 June. There followed a month of balance and counter-balance in which both sides attempted with little success to cut the other's lines of communication.

By late June, both armies faced each other in the area of the Gettysburg railhead. The Union forces enjoyed the advantage of the ridge of high ground to the south of the town, but the Confederates were better placed to take the offensive. The Texan Brigade, as part of Hood's Division and Longstreet's Corps, was positioned on the extreme right of the Confederate line facing III Corps led by Federal General Sickles. Denied the eyes and ears of Stuart's cavalry still some miles away on a fruitless foraging expedition, Lee lacked information on the terrain and enemy dispositions and was therefore unable to formulate a complete tactical plan.

On 1 July 1863, believing the main enemy defensive line to be further north than it was, Lee ordered Longstreet with two divisions (Hood on the right and McLaws on the left) to move south under cover of dead ground and thereafter to turn and advance north, rolling up the Federal flank in his path. Ironically, Sickles, in contravention of orders and against all military logic, had moved the leading elements of his corps forward to high ground in the path of the intended advance and now commanded the strategically important high ground north of the Round Tops. When Longstreet reached the forming-up point for his assault, he realized to his horror that instead of facing an understrength regiment supported by a battery of guns as he had anticipated, an entire corps now blocked his advance. Longstreet immediately requested permission to call off the attack, but permission was denied, and at approximately 4:00 p.m., Hood's Division attacked toward the Round Tops.

The four regiments of the Texas Brigade did all humanly possible to drive the Federals from their vantage point. The 1st Texas and 3rd Arkansas assailed the Devil's Den, a craggy promontory a little to the west of the Round Tops, while the 4th and 5th Texans supported Evander Law's Alabama Brigade in an assault on Little Round Top itself. At one stage, the Southerners reached the summit of the hill only to be slaughtered by the massed guns of Smith's 4th New York Battery, firing into them at point blank range. Eventually, exhausted and cut to pieces, the remnants of Longstreet's Corps, including the brave Texans, were forced by the sheer weight of enemy firepower to retire, leaving the Federal's much battered left flank intact.

No one was fully aware of it at the time, but on 2 July 1863, the Confederacy had reached its high water mark. The battle raged all that day and for another, but eventually Lee was forced to retreat and ultimately to retire southward into the safety of Virginia. Yet Hood's Texan Brigade could not have done more. In the words of Private Giles of the 4th Texas: "Every fellow [in the battle for the Little Round Top] was his own general. Private soldiers gave commands as loud as the officers; nobody paying any attention to either."

Texans were as independent in their dress as they were in all matters relating to discipline or regulations, and it was some time before the Texan Brigade adopted a universal uniform. Until then, all wore gray although the cut and shade varied greatly. Many wore frock coats, some with stripes across the chest in the manner of the Mississippi regiments, and most sported kepis. As the blockade took effect and replacement kit became more difficult to obtain, slouch hats of every color and design began to replace the kepis, while items of civilian wear and looted Federal equipment became more prevalent. As if to emphasize Texas' unique status as a previously independent republic, many of the troops displayed "Lone Stars" prominently on their pouches, headdress, and buckles.

CONFEDERATE STATE ARTILLERY

A battery of Confederate 12-pounder Napoleons captured at Missionary Ridge. The South could ill afford the loss of such magnificent weapons.

During the heady days of mass enlistment in the summer of 1861, few of the tens of thousands of Southerners who flocked to the newly raised Confederate colors considered service in the artillery. Spurred on by the reassuring presence of their friends and neighbors, most joined the local infantry battalions. Others who could ride, and who owned a suitable mount, favored the cavalry. Only a few ex-regular soldiers with previous gunnery experience willingly volunteered for the artillery.

Such batteries as were formed were usually neither numbered nor lettered but instead were generally identified by their commander's name. Others were either called after the area in which they were formed or were dedicated to a local hero. This led to confusion and did little to enhance a feeling of national identity among the gunners. Commanders were elected, invariably from among the social elite who, uniquely among the Southerners who fought in the War between the States, regarded service with the guns as prestigious.

Lee showed his disdain for artillery in 1862 by leaving the majority of his guns behind when embarking upon his invasion of the North. Nevertheless, after the Battle of Chancellorsville, he was forced to concede the necessity for massed artillery

and, in 1863, ordered a general reorganization of the 66 batteries within the Army of Northern Virginia. The six batteries of horse artillery were formed into a single battalion, although, thereafter, they rarely fought as such. The remaining artillery was grouped into 15 battalions of four batteries; each battalion being commanded by a lieutenant colonel with a major as second in command. Two or three battalions, when grouped together, were commanded by a colonel. Five battalions, under the command of a brigadier general, comprised a division, one of which was allotted to each of the three army corps. Within each corps, one battalion was allocated to each of the three infantry divisions. The remaining two, under the command of a colonel, formed the reserve.

Despite this reorganization, the battery, not the battalion, remained the pivot of Confederate artillery. For example, the men of Lieutenant Colonel Carter's battalion attached to Rodes's Division of II Corps continued to regard themselves as belonging to four strictly independent entities: Carter's Virginia Battery (King William Artillery), Fry's Virginia Battery (Orange Artillery), Page's Virginia Battery (Morris Artillery), and Reese's Alabama Battery (Jefferson Davis Artillery).

Headdress: Conventional Confederate gray kepis adorned with a red cap band and cover were worn by all enlisted gunners.

Jacket: Although many gunners retained the traditional double-breasted frock coat others favored the simpler shell jacket.

Webbing: Issue Confederate haversacks designed to carry ammunition forward proved unpopular and were often replaced by looted Federal-issue waterproof leather bags. Swords were issued to all gunners but were often abandoned as impractical.

Longstreet's Artillery
enfilading the Union
ordnance during the
Second Battle of Bull Run
(Manassas).

Most batteries were either self-financing or were sponsored by the regions from which they took their names. As the blockade bit deeper, horses, limbers, and accouterments became virtually impossible to obtain, necessitating the reduction in size of most batteries from six guns to four. Losses from counter-battery fire and from enemy snipers armed with the latest generation of long-range rifled muskets were occasionally so great that infantry companies were transferred *en masse* to serve the guns. None of this helped to preserve the *élan* usually associated with artillery regiments, with the result that traditional pride in unit, which so often manifested itself through smart appearance and discipline, was as a rule sadly lacking.

Distinctive items of dress which had originally served to give the individual batteries an air of independence were often abandoned as impractical after a few weeks in the field. Most batteries resorted to orthodox Confederate dress adorned with red chevrons and a red band around the kepi. Ironically, many photographs of enlisted men show them wearing regulation double-breasted frock coats long after these had become a rarity in other branches of service. When required, gunners would secure a primer pouch to their leather belts, in which they would store the friction primers needed to fire the cannon. Others would carry haversacks slung across their shoulders in which they would transport the heavy shells from the limber to the gun. Confederate haversacks were made of white cotton or drill and, at about 11 inches (28cm) square, were virtually useless for the needs of the gunners, most of whom abandoned them at the first opportunity in favor of plundered waterproof leather Federal-issue bags.

All ranks in the artillery were issued with swords, although most found these so heavy and impractical that they discarded them. The majority of swords in the South were of domestic manufacture although a number were imported from Europe and others were captured from the North. Locally produced items were of poor quality. Grips were often wrapped in oilcloth or brown leather secured by a single or, at best, double strand of untwisted copper or brass; hilts were crudely cast, and scabbards badly stiched. Short broad-bladed stabbing swords, no more than 18 inches (46cm) long and therefore of particular use in the tight confines of a battery position, became popular with those who could acquire them from civilian sources. Muskets were rare, although pistols, particularly copies of the ubiquitous Colt, were carried by all officers and a sizeable number of the men.

A few elite units retained high standards of discipline and dress throughout the war. Rutlidge's Battery, raised in Nashville, Tennessee in May 1861, later became Battery "A" of the 1st Tennessee Light Artillery, at which time its commander, Captain A.M. Rutlidge, was assigned to General Polk's staff. Seeing action at Mills Spring and Shiloh, the battery's losses in the latter engagement were so heavy that it was found necessary to amalgamate it with McClure's Battery. Despite its subordination, its losses, and its subsequent merger, it never completely lost its identity, and to the end, its members continued to wear their distinctive battery letter "A" on their collars and the crossed cannon barrels on their shoulders and hats.

Without doubt the most famous artillery unit to fight for the Confederate cause was the Washington Artillery. Organized in 1838 as the "Native American Battery" (Company "A" of Persifal Smith's Regiment), it fought with distinction in the Mexican War. Reorganized in 1852 as the Washington Artillery of New Orleans, its new recruits consisted entirely of wealthy and prominent citizens of that city. In 1857, command passed to Colonel J.B. Walton who did much to improve its standards. Under the command of Judah Benjamin, it offered its services to the Confederacy and was mustered in on 26 May 1861. The unit was fortunate to receive much of its equipment, including six 6–pounder cannon with ammunition, from the seizure of Baton Rouge Arsenal on 11 April 1861.

Four batteries of the Washington Artillery fought with the Army of Northern Virginia, helping to turn the tide during the 1st Battle of Manassas (Bull Run), and another fought with the Army of Tennessee. The Washington Artillery particularly distinguished itself in the defense of Marye's Heights during both the Fredericksburg and Chancellorsville campaigns. Commanded successively by Walton, Benjamin Eshelman, and William Miller Owen (the author of the emotive *A Hot Day on Marye's Heights*), the battalion, as it later became, fought in every major battle contested by the Army of Northern Virginia.

It is perhaps indicative of the Confederate attitude toward commissioning through the ranks that, despite their obvious social and academic advantages, few soldiers from this quite outstanding battalion were commissioned and posted elsewhere.

After the war, in a unique recognition of its fighting ability it was given permission by the victorious Federal government to form the "Washington Artillery Veterans Charitable & Benevolent Association Inc." Using this organization as a cover, it held secret drills, assembled weapons, and, in 1870, "rose" to drive the carpetbaggers and their supporters among Longstreet's Metropolitan Police off the streets. In later years, the Washington Artillery sent a battery to fight in Cuba during the Spanish-American War, and served with distinction in both World Wars.

The Washington Artillery wore distinctive blue uniforms, officers having frock coats and other ranks shell jackets. In line with both Federal and Confederate practice, a distinguishing red trim was worn on the upper part of the kepi, on the jacket trim, and along the seams of the trousers. Other ranks wore pipe-clayed leather belts, their head-dress bearing crossed-barrel cannon badges with the letters "WA" in brass. Officers wore a broad red sash with the bobble secured on the left, red epaulettes with gold edging, and conventional gold patterning on the lower sleeves. There were other Confederate artillery units that also bore the name "Washington Artillery." Captain G.H. Walter's South Carolina Artillery (Company "A" the Hampton Legion), Captain P.W. Bibb's Tennessee Artillery (the Washington or Hampton Artillery, although originally called Company "K" the 32nd Virginia Infantry and later Company "A" the 1st Virginia Artillery) and finally the Washington Mounted Artillery (Company "A" the 7th Battalion South Carolina Infantry) all aspired to the name. None, however, could match the original unit for panache, professionalism, and sheer determination.

The storming of the Confederate guns during the Battle of Nashville.

THE CONFEDERATE NAVY

At the outbreak of war, the Confederacy had neither a fleet nor a naval tradition. It did, however, have a long and vulnerable coastline liable to attack or blockade and an enemy increasingly reliant on imports from Europe. In 1860, John B. Floyd, the pro-secessionist U.S. Secretary of the Navy, sent the majority of the ships under his command on lengthy goodwill flag tours as far from their home bases as possible to give the South the opportunity to mobilize her limited naval resources without retaliation. When, on 16 March 1861, the Confederate government ordered the creation of a fleet to harry Northern commerce, Washington was able to do little to prevent it. By late 1864, when the Confederate force was at its zenith, the fleet numbered 700 commissioned and warrant officers, 3,674 enlisted men, and a land brigade formed specifically for the defense of Richmond. Due to its lack of raw materials and shipbuilding facilities, the South concentrated on quality rather than quantity. She built a total of 37 ironclads, including the revolutionary *Virginia* (*Merrimac*), (see p.59) and is generally considered to have had a far superior fleet of coastal sloops.

Appointed Confederate Secretary of the Navy on 21 February 1861, Stephen Mallory acted tirelessly throughout the war to insure that the Confederate fleet operated as efficiently as possible. Born in Jamaica but raised in Florida, Mallory qualified in the law, was appointed a judge at an early age, fought in the Seminole War, and served in the U.S. Senate until his resignation in 1861 upon the secession of his adopted state. He quickly realized that the motley collection of volunteers who were coming forward to man his new ships were simply too inexperienced to operate the privateers with which he intended to harass the Northern merchantmen on the high seas. Offering the command of these ships to the few seasoned seamen available, many of them foreign sympathizers, he retained the majority of his new recruits for the defense of his home waters.

As if to emphasize the lack of naval tradition within the Confederacy, several of the constituent states initially recruited their own naval forces. Virginia was the first to create a state navy, dressing it in conventional Federal uniform save for the inclusion of Commonwealth of Virginia buttons. Georgia followed suit soon after. Its officers, too, were issued with standard blue Federal uniforms with state buttons, but the sailors were more strikingly attired. Volunteers received a red flannel shirt with a sky blue falling collar and cuffs, both edged with white, conventional navy blue trousers,

15-inch Radman guns played a key role in Federal coastal defense. As the war progressed, many of the crews were transferred to light guns and sent to the front.

Headddress: Straw hats were initially issued to members of the Mobile Squadron as a concession to the heat, but were later tolerated in all commands.

Badges of rank: Rank and service were indicated by shoulder straps rather than by the more conventional epaulette rings favored by the North.

Weapons: Officers were issued with French-made Le Mats or domestically-produced Colt pistols. Deck officers often supplemented these with a British Royal Navy-pattern cutlass.

and a dark blue vizorless cap. Both forces were merged into the Confederate navy within months of their inception, as a result of which the apparent impracticality of the Georgian uniform was never put to the test.

Brought into being specifically for the defense of the Mississippi River, the Louisiana state navy lasted somewhat longer, commissioning its own ships and retaining its independence well into the war. Initially, officers and men were dressed in Federal blue, although later, gray double-breasted jackets were issued to certain officers.

Uniforms worn by the Confederate navy were initially similar to those of their Union opponents, save for the badges of rank which, in the case of officers, comprised gold stripes worn on the cuff. Until the introduction of formal regulations in 1862, sailors tended to dress for comfort. Thereafter

all wore new standard steel gray uniforms, necessitated by the inability of the South to obtain sufficient quantities of indigo to dye the cloth blue. Dress for a flag officer was declared to be "a frock coat of steel gray cloth, faced with the same and lined with black silk serge, double breasted, with two rows of large navy buttons on the breast, nine in each row, placed four inches and a half (11.5cm) apart from eye to eye at top, and two inches and a half (6.3cm) at bottom. Rolling collar, skirts to be full, commencing at the top of the hip bone and descending four-fifths thence toward the knee, with one button behind on each hip and one near the bottom of each fold. The cuffs to be two inches and a half deep, with one strip of gold lace one-half an inch (1.2cm) wide below the seam, but joining it." Three strips of lace, the uppermost to contain a 3-inch (7.5cm) loop, were to adorn the sleeve above the cuff. Captains were to

David torpedoes sit disarmed and harmless, a mute memorial to earlier, more violent, days.

wear a similar jacket without the gold stripes on the cuffs. All officers were to wear a steel gray or white single-breasted vest with a single row of nine small buttons and a standing collar as well as steel gray or white drill trousers spread loose to cover the boot or shoe.

Caps were to be between $3\frac{1}{2}$ and 4 inches (9–10cm) tall with a patent leather peak and gold band. Cap badges consisted of a fouled anchor within a wreath, with rank indicated by stars above the anchor: four for a flag officer reducing to one for a lieutenant. Plain wreaths were worn by midshipmen, assistant surgeons, and paymasters. Engineers wore an Old English letter "E" within the wreath, while, from June 1863, volunteer officers wore the plain gilt letters "VN" on their cap fronts.

Rank and service were indicated by shoulder straps. Flag officers were ordered to wear "straps of sky-blue cloth, edged with black, four inches (10cm) long and one inch and three-eighths (3.5cm) wide, bordered with an embroidery of gold one-quarter of an inch (65mm) in width, with four stars in line at equal distances, the two on the ends six-tenths of an inch (1.5cm) in diameter, and the two intermediate six-eighths of an inch (1.9cm) in diameter." Lesser officers wore a similar configuration except that captains wore only three stars ("six-tenths of an inch in diameter"), commanders two stars, and lieutenants one.

Perhaps inevitably, as the war progressed and uniforms became more difficult to maintain, standards dropped. As a concession to the heat, officers in the Mobile Squadron were allowed to relinquish their formal attire in favor of gray flannel frock or sack coats during the summer months, while straw hats were eventually tolerated among all ranks.

Boatswain's mates, gunner's mates, carpenter's mates, sailmaker's mates, ship's stewards and ship's cooks wore an embroidered fouled anchor of black silk, no more than 3 inches (7.5cm) long, on the right sleeve, and all other petty officers wore a similar device on the left, but in every other respect, they dressed in the same manner as the ordinary seaman. Under normal conditions, they wore gray cloth jackets and trousers or gray woolen frocks with white duck cuffs and collars, black hats, black silk neckerchiefs, and black shoes or boots. Thick gray caps without vizors were to be worn as an optional extra while at sea. In hot weather, each captain could, at his discretion, allow his crew to discard part or all of the thick outer uniform while on the high seas.

By 1863, most sailors seem to have been issued with a full set of regulation gear. However, since virtually all elements of their uniform, notably the ornate black buttons, were produced in Britain, it is likely that replacement equipment became increasingly difficult to obtain as the blockade tightened and the Confederacy coffers diminished. As a result, toward the end of the war Southern seamen were no better dressed than their infantry equivalents.

Weapons issued to the navy were varied, a symptom of the South's difficulty in obtaining munitions *en masse*. Seamen were issued with a 2-inch (5cm) thick buff leather belt held together by a standard loop and eyelet. Where relevant, fuzes and cartridges were carried in leather pouches attached to the belt and overstamped with a fouled anchor and crossed cannon. In 1861, 1,000 British Enfield P1858 naval rifles were purchased, and these were subsequently supplemented by an undisclosed number of British 0.54 caliber breechloading rifle-muskets. Either Colt revolvers or French-made Le Mats, with their nine-round 0.42 caliber chambers, were issued to officers, senior ratings, and boarding parties, while ordinary seamen were given a variety of cutlasses, usually either of Royal navy or Federal Model 1841 pattern, when deemed necessary.

THE CONFEDERATE PRIVATEER AND BLOCKADE RUNNER

On 17 April 1861, the President of the Confederate States issued a proclamation inviting "all those who may desire" to aid the Confederate cause by service in "private armed vessels." Interested persons received "letters of marque and reprisal" or were commissioned into the embryonic Confederate navy. Captains were told to furnish details of name, type, and tonnage of their ships, together with the intended number of the crew. Ordinary sailors were neither induced into the regular navy nor given a uniform. Pay was not offered, although there was the promise of lucrative prize money if they were successful.

Not all privateers actively pursued enemy shipping. The crews of a number of smaller craft made small fortunes during the winters of 1861 and 1862 by transporting bales of compressed cotton from the blockaded ports of the South to the "neutral" islands of the British West Indies, returning with all manner of contraband, from armaments to uniforms.

Many of the ships employed in this way were European-built side-wheel steamers designed primarily for passenger transportation across the English Channel. Most displaced between 400 and 600 tons and were propelled by feathering paddles. They had one or two raking telescopic funnels which could be lowered close to the deck, as well as two short lower masts, but no yardarms. The sides, which rarely stood more than a few feet above sea level, were invariably painted dull gray or lead and, as such, were virtually invisible to the naked eye at ranges in excess of 200 yards (183m). Many carried a "turtle-back" construction on the foredeck to enable them to weather heavy seas. Initially, smokeless domestic anthracite was burned, but when this became impossible to obtain, semi-bituminous Welsh coal was substituted. Of light

The *Florida* (formerly the *Oreto*) chases the *Star of Peace*.

Uniform: Privateers, although protected by Confederate "Letters of Marque," were not members of the armed forces and did not therefore wear uniform. Indeed many were not even American citizens, the crew of the *Alabama* being drawn almost exclusively from Liverpool.

Weapons: Personal weapons were privately purchased from a variety of sources. Inevitably cutlasses and pistols proved most popular, particularly among the deckhands who had occasionally to resort to boarding enemy ships to secure their capture.

The Confederate privateer *Alabama* was sunk by the U.S.S. *Kearsage* on 19 June 1864.

draft yet capable of considerable speed, such ships experienced little initial difficulty in outrunning the cumbersome cruisers and frigates of the blockading force. Using their considerable knowledge of the local waters, the captains invariably ran the Federal gauntlet late on moonless nights, relying on the element of surprise coupled with the inadequacy of Federal gunnery to keep them safe. As the war continued and the Union control of the Gulf of Mexico and the Caribbean tightened, short-range blockade running became more hazardous, but by then, many captains had made their fortunes.

Many of the ships which carried the cotton onward from the West Indies to Liverpool were Confederate owned but British crewed. It has even been suggested that several Royal navy officers took lengthy leaves of absence to offer their services (under assumed names) to the Confederacy, although exact details remain a mystery and none was ever captured.

The commerce-destroyers, the true privateers, ventured much farther from the protection of their own coastline. In 1861, the United States boasted a mercantile fleet second only to that of Britain in tonnage. After secession, 90 percent of it remained loyal to the Union and immediately became the target of Southern cruisers and armed merchantmen. Washington argued that the use of privateers in war was contrary to the terms of the Declaration of the Congress of Paris of 1856. When it was pointed out by a far from neutral Britain that the United States had earlier refused to become a signatory to the Declaration, Washington offered belatedly to accede but was refused leave to do so. Privateering therefore remained a bona fide act of war in the eyes of all but the Union, which threatened to treat captured Confederate privateers as pirates.

In a proclamation of 19 April 1861, Lincoln stated that if "any person under the pretended authority of the said States, or under any other pretence, shall molest a vessel of the United States, or the persons or cargo on board her, such person will be held amenable to the laws of the United States for the prevention and punishment of piracy." Although crews which fell into Federal hands were often tried and occasionally convicted, none was ever punished for fear of Confederate retaliation against Union prisoners of war then swelling Southern prison camps.

During the first year of the war, privateers met with limited success. A fleet of small boats, ranging from old slavers to tugs, from fishing schooners to revenue cutters – in fact, anything big enough to carry a large piece of ordnance – were fitted out and placed strategically along the coast of the Carolinas from where they preyed upon unsuspecting Federal coastal shipping. Cargos were seized and ships pressed into service to replace those which inevitably fell foul of powerful blockading cruisers.

The lives of privateering ships were generally short. The brig *Jeff Davis*, a one-time slaver, spent a few months successfully apprehending prizes off New England, but it was eventually wrecked off the coast of Florida. The Charleston schooner *Beauregard* was overhauled and captured by the Federal barque *W.G. Anderson*. The schooner *Judah* was burned at her wharf in the Pensicola (Florida) naval yard by a landing party from the U.S.S. *Colorado*, while the former revenue cutter *Petrel* was sunk by a shell from the frigate *St. Lawrence* as the Southern craft was cruising off Charleston. The capture of the 54-ton Charleston pilot boat *Savannah* by the brig *Perry* nearly led to a diplomatic incident when the crew were taken to New York and tried for piracy, but the threat of retaliation against prisoners in Southern hands forced the North to reconsider.

Tempers were not so easily placated when Mason and Slidell, two Confederate commissioners tasked with the purchase of ships and materials in Britain, were forcibly taken from the British mail steamer *Trent* by Captain Wilkes of the U.S.S. *San Jacinto* while on the high seas. The commissioners were quickly returned to British jurisdiction, but not before immeasurable harm had been done to the Union cause in the eyes of the world's neutrals.

As the war progressed, the task of the small privateer became much more dangerous, forcing many of the remaining captains into the more lucrative and safer world of blockade running. In response, the Confederacy turned to Britain for the provision of a number of new ships. Negotiations invariably took place through a series of foreign-based intermediaries to avoid prosecution under the neutrality laws, but there can be no doubt that the ultimate destination of the ships was an open secret.

The Florida, the first of the commerce-destroyers of British origin, typified the subterfuge. Built in Liverpool during the winter of 1861–62, ostensibly for the Italian government (which strenuously denied all knowledge of her), she was initially named *Oreto*. She was allowed to leave Liverpool on 22 March 1862 from where she headed, not to Palermo as stated on her Bills of Lading, but to Jamaica. At about the same time, the guns and munitions for the new cruiser were shipped in the steamer *Bahama* to Nassau from the British eastern port of Hartlepool. Immediately upon her arrival in Nassau on 28 April, the *Oreto* was consigned to Messrs. Adderly & Co., the local agents for Messrs. Fraser, Trenholm & Co. of Liverpool, who were financial agents for the Confederate government. Command now passed to Captain Maffitt of the Confederate navy who at once sailed her to Cochrane's Anchorage, some nine miles from Nassau, where she took on small arms, ammunition, and her new crew. Spurred on by formal and accurate Union complaints, the British government at last intervened but, after a few weeks, allowed the ship to continue on her way. On 7 August, the now renamed *Florida* sailed to the deserted island of Green Cay in the Bahamas where she trans-shipped her battery of two 7-inch (18cm) rifles and six 6-inch (15cm) guns. Once ready, and now a fully fledged warship openly flying the flag of the Confederate navy, the *Florida* sailed for the safety of a home base.

The second and more famous cruiser, the *Alabama*, sailed from Liverpool on 23 June 1862. Despite the greatest protestations from the U.S. ambassador in London, Charles Adams, the British government refused to prevent the ship from leaving harbor on a test voyage, from which it never returned. She was provisioned with guns, ammunition, and coal in the Azores and placed under the command of Captain Raphael Semmes of the Confederate navy. Although at this stage, the civilian crew was given ample opportunity to return to Liverpool, most had enlisted in the full knowledge of the ship's status and, in the hopes of prize money, readily agreed to continue the voyage. *Alabama* therefore became a Confederate ship with a Southern captain but an almost exclusively British crew. The cruiser was defeated and sunk by the U.S.S. *Kearsarge* off the French port of Cherbourg on 19 June 1864, but not until she herself had sunk, burned, or captured 69 Federal ships, including the U.S.S. *Hatteras*.

Despite Union protestations to the contrary, privateering has never been considered contrary to the laws of war and the captains and crews of such ships as the *Savannah* and the *Alabama* therefore committed no crime. Indeed many, particularly those engaged in the early stages of the war before the Union blockade became effective, made small fortunes. According to "A. Roberts" (probably the *nom de guerre* of a British officer), at the end of a successful voyage a captain might have expected to make £1,000. Equally well paid were the pilot who might command £750, the chief engineer £500 and the chief and junior officers £250 and £150 respectively. Even the deckhands might expect £50, virtually enough on which to retire for life. It is no surprise, therefore, that the Confederacy found it so easy to fill the vacancies within its fleet of privateers with willing British seamen.

Captain John Newland Maffitt, commander of the *Florida*.

At the height of his raiding, Captain Semmes of the *Alabama* would tempt enemy ships towards him by setting fire to a prize ship and using it as a decoy.

THE CONFEDERATE MARINES

On 16 March 1861, the Confederate government authorized the creation of a Marine Corps consisting of a major, a quartermaster, a paymaster, an adjutant, a sergeant major, a quartermaster sergeant, and six companies, each with a captain, a first lieutenant, a second lieutenant, four sergeants, four corporals, 100 privates, and ten musicians. In all, over 1,600 officers and men served in the Corps throughout the war, although there were never more than 600 on active service at any one time. The Corps fought in all the major sea battles as well as in the defense of Richmond.

What is known about Marine Corps uniforms is extremely fragmentary, although several good photographs do exist to give a reasonable indication of what this small though élite unit wore.

Officers had French-style kepis covered in either blue or gray material, usually with black leather peaks and chinstraps. Coats were universally gray and of double-breasted frock coat design with twin rows of seven brass buttons each. Rank insignia were borrowed directly from the army. One, two, and three collar stripes were worn by second lieutenants to captains, one, two and three stars by majors to colonels. Gold Austrian knots were worn on the sleeve – one braid by lieutenants, two by captains, and three by field officers. A significant number of coats had dark blue collars and cuffs, a number had stiff white collar linings, and a few U.S. Marine Corps officers had gold Russian shoulder knots. Trousers were usually dark blue, although at least one officer is known to have favored sky blue with black welts down the outer seams.

Fatigue dress was even more informal. Most officers tried to emulate the naval personnel with whom they served by wearing blue jackets and white trousers while at sea. Others, however, seem to have preferred an all-gray mode of dress. Although formal dress regulations did exist, particularly for shore-based companies, these seem to have been introduced relatively late in the war, by which time the majority of officers had purchased their own variations of uniforms, and, by all accounts, the regulations were largely ignored.

Uniforms for the enlisted men were purchased in bulk in England and were therefore far more consistent with dress regulations. Marines were issued with gray felt fatigue caps with black peaks and chinstraps and brass side buttons, and two uniform coats and four fatigue jackets, all universally gray. Both coats and jackets appear to have been worn, particularly by the Naval Brigade which took part in the defense of Richmond, although the longer frock coat seems to have been the more common.

The bombardment of Fort Sumter from Fort Moultrie on 12–13 April 1861 led to the formal commencement of hostilities.

Headddress: All ranks wore a black-peaked blue kepi adorned in the case of officers with gold piping.

Frock coat: Officers wore standard gray double-breasted frock coats with the badges of rank edged in red.

Weapons: A variety of weapons was carried. The officer in the foreground is armed with a Le Mat revolver and a navy variant of an infantry officer's sword, the Marine behind probably with a British 1853-pattern Enfield.

Seven buttons, each bearing the Roman letter "M" were fitted. Rank was indicated by black chevrons worn point up. Two chevrons indicated a corporal, three a sergeant, three with a diamond a first sergeant, three with ties a quartermaster sergeant, and three with arcs a sergeant major.

Trousers were dark blue for winter and white cotton for summer. Gray or blue outer shirts were occasionally worn in hot weather, but at other times, a white shirt was worn under the jacket.

The vast majority of Marines served on one of the regular, commissioned naval vessels. The *Sumter*, the first such craft, was originally a screw steamer of some 500 tons designed specifically to ply for trade between New Orleans and Havana. Prior to commissioning, her frame was strengthened, a berth deck added, the spar deck cabins removed, and space found for a magazine and additional coal bunkers. She was armed with an 8-inch (20cm) pivot gun before the fore and main masts, and four 24-pound howitzers in her broadside.

The highly experienced Captain Semmes (see p.151) was placed in command on 18 April 1861 with orders to sail at once for the open sea before the Union blockade could take effect. However, the *Sumter* could not be made ready until 18 June, by which time a sizeable Union flotilla consisting of the *Brooklyn*, *Powhatan*, Massachusetts, and *South Carolina* was standing off in readiness to meet her. Relying heavily upon local intelligence, Semmes brought his ship to a state of immediate readiness and waited for one of the blockade ships to leave station. After two weeks of frustration, news arrived that the *Brooklyn* had left her designated post to chase a Southern merchantman. Seizing his opportunity, Semmes immediately put to sea and within hours was free of the pursuing enemy.

When only three days out, the *Sumter* made her first kill when she overhauled and burned the barque *Golden Rocket*, and within one week of escaping the blockade, she had captured seven other merchantmen. One was ordered to New Orleans with a prize crew but was captured by a Union cruiser before reaching the safety of the Mississippi. The others were sailed to Cienfuegos on the southern coast of Cuba, from where they were eventually released into Federal hands by the nervous Spanish authorities. During the next two months, the *Sumter* cruised in the Caribbean and along the coast of South America, frequently putting into neutral ports for coaling and provisioning. At no time did the neutral harbor authorities refuse her assistance and only on one occasion, at Puerto Cabello in Venezuela, was she forced to leave after 48 hours, pursuant to the terms and conditions of the international neutrality laws. Fearful of the number of Federal warships chasing him (there were, in fact, six), Semmes now made for the quieter waters of the western Atlantic, where he overhauled and burned two more merchantmen.

After two months' cruising in the Atlantic, Semmes was forced to put into St. Pierre, on the French-owned island of Martinique, for coal and water. At this point, his considerable luck seemed to run out. After only five days in harbor, the fast Federal sloop-of-war *Iroquois* sailed into view. Wary of France's rigid interpretation of the rules of neutrality, particularly that which forbade a warship to leave harbor within 24 hours of an enemy craft, Captain Palmer, in command of the *Iroquois*, immediately put to sea, anchored in the outer Sound and awaited events. There matters remained for a week.

On the night of 23 November, now fully prepared for battle, *Sumter* weighed anchor and stood out. Realizing that his every move would be signaled by Union schooners in port, Semmes attempted to trick his adversary by heading directly south and then doubling back under cover of the land. Aided by a fortuitous rain squall, he succeeded in giving Palmer the slip to the extent that, by daybreak, he was steaming at full speed to the north while the *Iroquois* was pursuing him fruitlessly in the opposite direction.

Temporarily free of her hunters, *Sumter* now

cruised eastward into the Atlantic, seizing and burning three prizes. Then the advent of unexpectedly bad weather forced Semmes to seek the protection of a neutral harbor to undertake a major refit. The Spanish port of Cadiz was chosen, but for once the harbor authorities showed a marked reluctance to allow the ship to stay. Semmes sailed for Gibraltar hoping to receive a more friendly reception at the hands of the British authorities, but instead found that neither the government nor local merchants would furnish him with coal or provisions. Due to the dilapidated state of the ship, serious consideration was given to the transfer of the officers and Marines to a new vessel. However, this desperate measure was pre-empted when the Federal warships *Tuscarora*, *Kearsage*, and *Ino* sailed into the Straits and immediately took up station at Algeciras ready to intercept the Confederate

cruiser as soon as she attempted to leave the protection of British territorial waters. Conscious of the hopelessness of the situation and in an attempt to avert needless bloodshed, *Sumter* remained at her berth, was decommissioned and ultimately sold. Ironically, she was later to reappear as a blockade runner.

During her cruise, *Sumter* had obtained 17 prizes. Of these, two were ransomed, seven released in Cuban ports by order of the Spanish authorities, and two recaptured. In all, *Sumter* burned six enemy vessels with their cargos – hardly a huge number when the size of the Federal mercantile fleet was taken into account. She did, however, tie up a considerable part of the Union's fleet of cruisers dispatched to hunt her down and may therefore be deemed to have been at least a qualified success.

The battle between *Monitor* and *Merrimac*, fought on 9 March 1862 at Hampton Roads, near Norfolk, Virginia.

BADGES OF RANK: C.S. ARMY

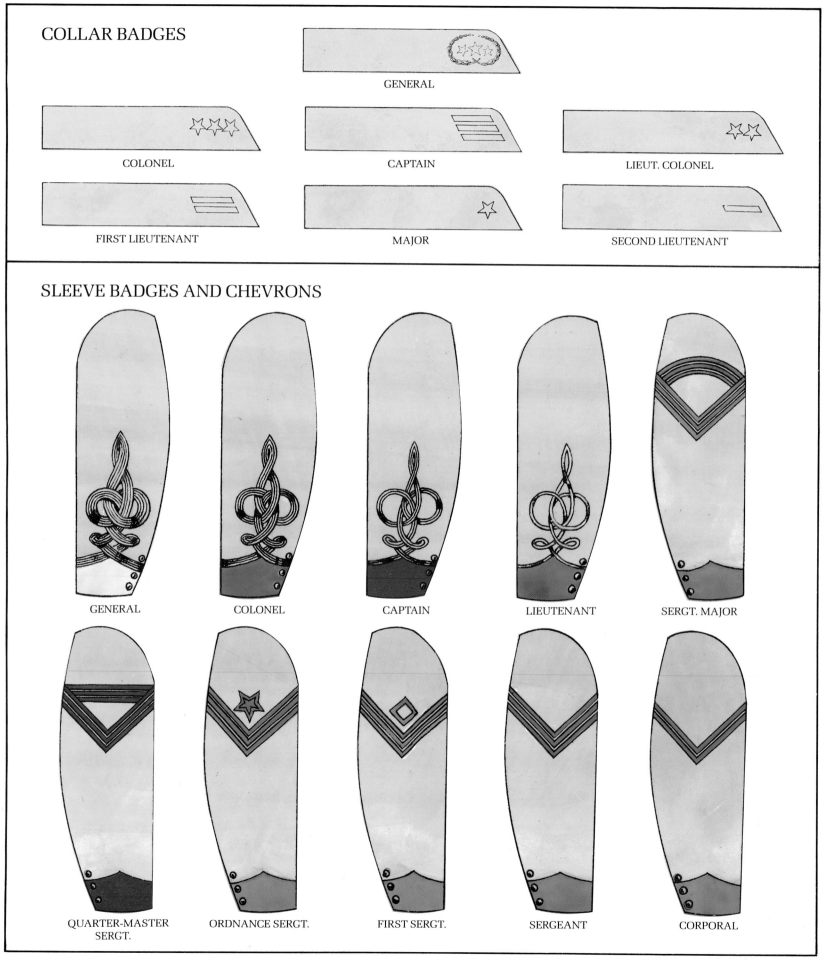

COLLAR BADGES

GENERAL

COLONEL

CAPTAIN

LIEUT. COLONEL

FIRST LIEUTENANT

MAJOR

SECOND LIEUTENANT

SLEEVE BADGES AND CHEVRONS

GENERAL

COLONEL

CAPTAIN

LIEUTENANT

SERGT. MAJOR

QUARTER-MASTER SERGT.

ORDNANCE SERGT.

FIRST SERGT.

SERGEANT

CORPORAL

Index

Acknowledgements
4 volume set (originally published as Combat
Uniforms of the Civil War)

Alabama Department of Archives and History,
Hulton Getty, Library of Congress, Museum of
the Confederacy, National Archives, North
Carolina State Division of Archives, Peter
Newark's Western Americana, Smithsonian
Institution, Texas State Library, Virginia
Military Institute.